Wonderful ways to prepare

SOUPS

by JO ANN SHIRLEY

OTHER TITLES IN THIS SERIES

1. HORS D'ŒUVRES & FIRST COURSES

2. SOUPS

3. MEAT

4. FISH & SEAFOOD

5. STEWS & CASSEROLES

6. SALADS

7. DESSERTS

8. CAKES & COOKIES

9. BARBECUES

10. ITALIAN FOOD

Printed in Canada.

Wonderful ways to prepare

SOUPS

PLAYMORE INC NEW YORK USA
UNDER ARRANGEMENT WITH
I, WALDMAN & SON INC

**AYERS & JAMES PTY LTD
CROWS NEST AUSTRALIA**

**STAFFORD PEMBERTON PUBLISHING
KNUTSFORD UNITED KINGDOM**

FIRST PUBLISHED 1978

PUBLISHED IN THE USA
BY PLAYMORE INC.
UNDER ARRANGEMENT WITH I. WALDMAN & SON INC.

PUBLISHED IN AUSTRALIA
BY AYERS & JAMES PTY. LTD.
CROWS NEST.   AUSTRALIA

PUBLISHED IN THE UNITED KINGDOM
BY STAFFORD PEMBERTON PUBLISHING
KNUTSFORD CHESIRE

ISBN 0 86908 055 5

OVEN TEMPERATURE GUIDE

Description	Gas		Electric		Mark
	C	F	C	F	
Cool	100	200	110	225	¼
Very Slow	120	250	120	250	½
Slow	150	300	150	300	1-2
Moderately slow	160	325	170	340	3
Moderate	180	350	200	400	4
Moderately hot	190	375	220	425	5-6
Hot	200	400	230	450	6-7
Very hot	230	450	250	475	8-9

LIQUID MEASURES

IMPERIAL	METRIC
1 teaspoon	5 ml
1 tablespoon	20 ml
2 fluid ounces (¼ cup)	62.5 ml
4 fluid ounces (½ cup)	125 ml
8 fluid ounces (1 cup)	250 ml
1 pint (16 ounces — 2 cups)*	500 ml

* (The imperial pint is equal to 20 fluid ounces.)

SOLID MEASURES

AVOIRDUPOIS	METRIC
1 ounce	30 g
4 ounces (¼ lb)	125 g
8 ounces (½ lb)	250 g
12 ounces (¾ lb)	375 g
16 ounces (1 lb)	500 g
24 ounces (1½ lb)	750 g
32 ounces (2 lb)	1000 g (1 kg)

CUP AND SPOON REPLACEMENTS FOR OUNCES

INGREDIENT	½ oz	1 oz	2 oz	3 oz	4 oz	5 oz	6 oz	7 oz	8 oz
Almonds, ground	2 T	¼ C	½ C	¾ C	1¼ C	1⅓ C	1⅔ C	2 C	2¼ C
slivered	6 t	¼ C	½ C	¾ C	1 C	1⅓ C	1⅔ C	2 C	2¼ C
whole	2 T	¼ C	⅓ C	½ C	¾ C	1 C	1¼ C	1⅓ C	1½ C
Apples, dried whole	3 T	½ C	1 C	1⅓ C	2 C	2⅓ C	2¾ C	3⅓ C	3¾ C
Apricots, chopped	2 T	¼ C	½ C	¾ C	1 C	1¼ C	1½ C	1¾ C	2 C
whole	2 T	3 T	½ C	⅔ C	1 C	1¼ C	1⅓ C	1½ C	1¾ C
Arrowroot	1 T	2 T	⅓ C	½ C	⅔ C	¾ C	1 C	1¼ C	1⅓ C
Baking Powder	1 T	2 T	⅓ C	½ C	⅔ C	¾ C	1 C	1 C	1¼ C
Baking Soda	1 T	2 T	⅓ C	½ C	⅔ C	¾ C	1 C	1 C	1¼ C
Barley	1 T	2 T	¼ C	½ C	⅔ C	¾ C	1 C	1 C	1¼ C
Breadcrumbs, dry	2 T	¼ C	½ C	¾ C	1 C	1¼ C	1½ C	1¾ C	2 C
soft	¼ C	½ C	1 C	1½ C	2 C	2½ C	3 C	3⅔ C	4¼ C
Biscuit Crumbs	2 T	¼ C	½ C	¾ C	1¼ C	1⅓ C	1⅔ C	2 C	2¼ C
Butter	3 t	6 t	¼ C	⅓ C	½ C	⅔ C	¾ C	1 C	1 C
Cheese, grated, lightly packed,									
natural cheddar	6 t	¼ C	½ C	¾ C	1 C	1¼ C	1½ C	1¾ C	2 C
Processed cheddar	5 t	2 T	⅓ C	⅔ C	¾ C	1 C	1¼ C	1½ C	1⅔ C
Parmesan, Romano	6 t	¼ C	½ C	¾ C	1 C	1⅓ C	1⅔ C	2 C	2¼ C
Cherries, candied, chopped	1 T	2 T	⅓ C	½ C	¾ C	1 C	1 C	1⅓ C	1½ C
whole	1 T	2 T	⅓ C	½ C	⅔ C	¾ C	1 C	1¼ C	1⅓ C
Cocoa	2 T	¼ C	½ C	¾ C	1¼ C	1⅓ C	1⅔ C	2 C	2¼ C
Coconut, desiccated	2 T	⅓ C	⅔ C	1 C	1⅓ C	1⅔ C	2 C	2⅓ C	2⅔ C
shredded	⅓ C	⅔ C	1¼ C	1¾ C	2½ C	3 C	3⅔ C	4⅓ C	5 C
Cornstarch	6 t	3 T	½ C	⅔ C	1 C	1¼ C	1½ C	1⅔ C	2 C
Corn Syrup	2 t	1 T	2 T	¼ C	⅓ C	½ C	½ C	⅔ C	⅔ C
Coffee, ground	2 T	⅓ C	⅔ C	1 C	1⅓ C	1⅔ C	2 C	2⅓ C	2⅔ C
instant	3 T	½ C	1 C	1⅓ C	1¾ C	2¼ C	2⅔ C	3 C	3½ C
Cornflakes	½ C	1 C	2 C	3 C	4¼ C	5¼ C	6¼ C	7⅓ C	8⅓ C
Cream of Tartar	1 T	2 T	⅓ C	½ C	⅔ C	¾ C	1 C	1 C	1¼ C
Currants	1 T	2 T	⅓ C	⅔ C	¾ C	1 C	1¼ C	1½ C	1⅔ C
Custard Powder	6 t	3 T	½ C	⅔ C	1 C	1¼ C	1½ C	1⅔ C	2 C
Dates, chopped	1 T	2 T	⅓ C	⅔ C	¾ C	1 C	1¼ C	1½ C	1⅔ C
whole, pitted	1 T	2 T	⅓ C	½ C	¾ C	1 C	1¼ C	1⅓ C	1½ C
Figs, chopped	1 T	2 T	⅓ C	½ C	¾ C	1 C	1 C	1⅓ C	1½ C
Flour, all-purpose or cake	6 t	¼ C	½ C	¾ C	1 C	1¼ C	1½ C	1¾ C	2 C
wholemeal	6 t	3 T	½ C	⅔ C	1 C	1¼ C	1⅓ C	1⅔ C	1¾ C
Fruit, mixed	1 T	2 T	⅓ C	½ C	¾ C	1 C	1¼ C	1⅓ C	1½ C
Gelatine	5 t	2 T	⅓ C	½ C	¾ C	1 C	1 C	1¼ C	1½ C
Ginger, crystallised pieces	1 T	2 T	⅓ C	½ C	¾ C	1 C	1¼ C	1⅓ C	1½ C
ground	6 t	⅓ C	½ C	¾ C	1¼ C	1½ C	1¾ C	2 C	2¼ C
preserved, heavy syrup	1 T	2 T	⅓ C	½ C	⅔ C	¾ C	1 C	1 C	1¼ C
Glucose, liquid	2 t	1 T	2 T	¼ C	⅓ C	½ C	½ C	⅔ C	⅔ C
Haricot Beans	1 T	2 T	⅓ C	½ C	⅔ C	¾ C	1 C	1 C	1¼ C

In this table, t represents teaspoonful, T represents tablespoonful and C represents cupful.

CUP AND SPOON REPLACEMENTS FOR OUNCES (Cont.)

INGREDIENT	½ oz	1 oz	2 oz	3 oz	4 oz	5 oz	6 oz	7 oz	8 oz
Honey	2 t	1 T	2 T	¼ C	⅓ C	½ C	½ C	⅔ C	⅔ C
Jam	2 t	1 T	2 T	¼ C	⅓ C	½ C	½ C	⅔ C	¾ C
Lentils	1 T	2 T	⅓ C	½ C	⅔ C	¾ C	1 C	1 C	1¼ C
Macaroni (see pasta)									
Milk Powder, full cream	2 T	¼ C	½ C	¾ C	1¼ C	1⅓ C	1⅔ C	2 C	2¼ C
non fat	2 T	⅓ C	¾ C	1¼ C	1½ C	2 C	2⅓ C	2¾ C	3¼ C
Nutmeg	6 t	3 T	½ C	⅔ C	¾ C	1 C	1¼ C	1½ C	1⅔ C
Nuts, chopped	6 t	¼ C	½ C	¾ C	1 C	1¼ C	1½ C	1¾ C	2 C
Oatmeal	1 T	2 T	½ C	⅔ C	¾ C	1 C	1¼ C	1½ C	1⅔ C
Olives, whole	1 T	2 T	⅓ C	⅔ C	¾ C	1 C	1¼ C	1½ C	1⅔ C
sliced	1 T	2 T	⅓ C	⅔ C	¾ C	1 C	1¼ C	1½ C	1⅔ C
Pasta, short (e.g. macaroni)	1 T	2 T	⅓ C	⅔ C	¾ C	1 C	1¼ C	1½ C	1⅔ C
Peaches, dried & whole	1 T	2 T	⅓ C	⅔ C	¾ C	1 C	1¼ C	1½ C	1⅔ C
chopped	6 t	¼ C	½ C	¾ C	1 C	1¼ C	1½ C	1¾ C	2 C
Peanuts, shelled, raw, whole	1 T	2 T	⅓ C	½ C	¾ C	1 C	1¼ C	1⅓ C	1½ C
roasted	1 T	2 T	⅓ C	⅔ C	¾ C	1 C	1¼ C	1½ C	1⅔ C
Peanut Butter	3 t	6 t	3 T	⅓ C	½ C	½ C	⅔ C	¾ C	1 C
Peas, split	1 T	2 T	⅓ C	½ C	⅔ C	¾ C	1 C	1 C	1¼ C
Peel, mixed	1 T	2 T	⅓ C	½ C	¾ C	1 C	1 C	1¼ C	1½ C
Potato, powder	1 T	2 T	¼ C	⅓ C	½ C	⅔ C	¾ C	1 C	1¼ C
flakes	¼ C	½ C	1 C	1⅓ C	2 C	2⅓ C	2¾ C	3⅓ C	3¾ C
Prunes, chopped	1 T	2 T	⅓ C	½ C	⅔ C	¾ C	1 C	1¼ C	1⅓ C
whole pitted	1 T	2 T	⅓ C	½ C	⅔ C	¾ C	1 C	1 C	1¼ C
Raisins	2 T	¼ C	⅓ C	½ C	¾ C	1 C	1 C	1⅓ C	1½ C
Rice, short grain, raw	1 T	2 T	¼ C	½ C	⅔ C	¾ C	1 C	1 C	1¼ C
long grain, raw	1 T	2 T	⅓ C	½ C	¾ C	1 C	1¼ C	1⅓ C	1½ C
Rice Bubbles	⅔ C	1¼ C	2½ C	3⅔ C	5 C	6¼ C	7½ C	8¾ C	10 C
Rolled Oats	2 T	⅓ C	⅔ C	1 C	1⅓ C	1¾ C	2 C	2½ C	2¾ C
Sago	2 T	¼ C	⅓ C	½ C	¾ C	1 C	1 C	1¼ C	1½ C
Salt, common	3 t	6 t	¼ C	⅓ C	½ C	⅔ C	¾ C	1 C	1 C
Semolina	1 T	2 T	⅓ C	½ C	¾ C	1 C	1 C	1⅓ C	1½ C
Spices	6 t	3 T	¼ C	⅓ C	½ C	½ C	⅔ C	¾ C	1 C
Sugar, plain	3 t	6 t	¼ C	⅓ C	½ C	⅔ C	¾ C	1 C	1 C
confectioners'	1 T	2 T	⅓ C	½ C	¾ C	1 C	1 C	1¼ C	1½ C
moist brown	1 T	2 T	⅓ C	½ C	¾ C	1 C	1 C	1⅓ C	1½ C
Tapioca	1 T	2 T	⅓ C	½ C	⅔ C	¾ C	1 C	1¼ C	1⅓ C
Treacle	2 t	1 T	2 T	¼ C	⅓ C	½ C	½ C	⅔ C	⅔ C
Walnuts, chopped	2 T	¼ C	½ C	¾ C	1 C	1¼ C	1½ C	1¾ C	2 C
halved	2 T	⅓ C	⅔ C	1 C	1¼ C	1½ C	1¾ C	2¼ C	2½ C
Yeast, dried	6 t	3 T	½ C	⅔ C	1 C	1¼ C	1⅓ C	1⅔ C	1¾ C
compressed	3 t	6 t	3 T	⅓ C	½ C	½ C	⅔ C	¾ C	1 C

In this table, t represents teaspoonful, T represents tablespoonful and C represents cupful.

Beef, Chicken and Vegetable Soup

2 medium onions, sliced
1 tablespoon (20 g) butter or
   margarine
2 lb (1 kg) chuck steak in one piece
1 medium chicken
2 lb (1 kg) beef soup bones
12 cups (3 liters) water
salt
2 bay leaves
8 whole black peppercorns
4 tablespoons chopped parsley
½ teaspoon thyme
2 whole cloves
1 cup diced celery
4 carrots, diced
3 leeks, sliced, white part only
¼ small cabbage, shredded
½ lb (250 g) peas
pepper
grated cheese

1. Saute onions in butter in a large saucepan.
2. Add beef, chicken, bones, water, 1 tablespoon salt, bay leaves, whole peppers, parsley, thyme and cloves. Bring to a boil. Reduce heat and simmer, covered, for 2-3 hours or until meats are tender.
3. Remove meats, cool and cut into bite-size pieces. Discard bones.
4. Cook celery, carrots, leeks, cabbage and peas until barely tender in a little boiling water. Drain.
5. Add vegetables to the soup.
6. Heat thoroughly.
7. Sprinkle with grated cheese.

Serves 8-10.

Cottage Cheese Soup

1 teaspoon celery seed
4 cups (1 liter) milk
1 tablespoon minced onion
3 tablespoons (60 g) butter
  or margarine
2 tablespoons flour
1¼ teaspoons salt

¼ teaspoon white pepper
½ teaspoon paprika
pinch nutmeg
2 cups cottage cheese
2 tablespoons minced pimiento
minced watercress

1. In top part of double boiler put celery and milk. Heat over simmering water for 15 minutes. Strain.
2. In a small saucepan saute the onion in the butter or margarine. Blend in flour and seasonings. Add milk and mix thoroughly. Return to top of double boiler and cook until thickened, stirring constantly.
3. Add cottage cheese, mix well and heat thoroughly.
4. Serve garnished with pimiento and watercress.

Serves 4.

Eggplant Soup

1 lb (500 g) meat, fish
  or chicken
2 tablespoons (40 g) butter
  or margarine
1 medium onion, quartered

½ lb (250 g) tomatoes
1 lb (500 g) eggplant
7½ cups (1.8 liters) water
1 teaspoon salt
½ teaspoon pepper

1. Cut meat into bite-size pieces.
2. In a large saucepan, melt the butter and saute the onions, tomatoes and eggplant until tender. Add salt.
3. Remove vegetables and put through a sieve or purée in an electric blender.
4. Add the water to the meat.
5. Add puréed vegetables and cook until meat is tender.
6. Season to taste with salt and pepper.

Serves 4-6.

Fish and Cheese Soup

1½ lb (750 g) white fish fillets	½ cup flour
3 tablespoons (60 g) butter	¼ teaspoon paprika
or margarine	½ teaspoons salt
1 stalk celery, chopped	5 cups (1.2 liters) chicken stock
1 large onion, chopped	4 cups (1 liter) milk
1 carrot, diced	⅔ cup (185 g) grated cheese

1. Cut fish into bite-size pieces.
2. Melt the butter or margarine in saucepan and saute the celery, onion, and carrot until tender.
3. Remove from heat and stir in flour, paprika and salt.
4. Stirring constantly, add milk and chicken stock.
5. Simmer until thick and creamy, stirring constantly.
6. Add fish pieces and bring to a boil. Reduce heat and simmer, stirring occasionally, for 10-15 minutes.
7. Add cheese and stir until melted.
8. Sprinkle a little paprika on the top of each serving.

Serves 8.

Hot Cucumber Soup

1 lb (500 g) cucumbers	4 cups (1 liter) chicken stock
2 tablespoons (40 g) butter	salt and pepper
or margarine	1 tablespoon lemon juice
1 large onion, chopped	1 tablespoon chopped mint
4 tablespoons flour	½ cup (125 ml) cream

1. Peel and slice the cucumbers.
2. Melt the butter or margarine in a large saucepan and saute the onion until transparent.
3. Stir in the flour. Add the stock and bring to a boil.
4. Add the sliced cucumber and cook until tender.
5. Sieve or purée in an electric blender. Season to taste with salt and pepper. Stir in lemon juice.
6. Return to saucepan and reheat.
7. Just before serving, mix in the chopped mint and the cream.

Serves 4.

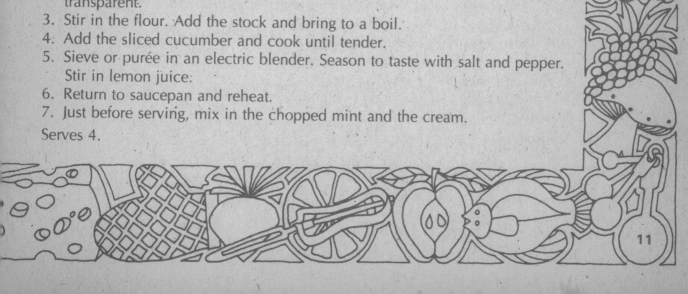

Hungarian Soup

2 medium onions, chopped
2 tablespoons (40 g) butter
  or margarine
2 lb (1 kg) stewing beef
½ lb (250 g) beef liver
2½ teaspoons salt
2 teaspoons paprika

2 green peppers, sliced
2 tomatoes, sliced
1 carrot, diced
1 tablespoon chopped parsley
6 cups (1.5 liters) water
2 potatoes, diced

1. Saute onions in butter or margarine in a heavy saucepan.
2. Cut beef and liver into bite-size pieces and add to onions. Saute until well browned.
3. Add salt, paprika, pepper, tomatoes, carrot, parsley and water.
4. Bring to a boil. Reduce heat and simmer until meat is tender. Add more water if necessary.
5. Add diced potatoes and cook for another ½ hour or until potatoes are cooked.

Serves 6.

Buttermilk Soup

7½ cups (1.8 liters) buttermilk
3 tablespoons chopped chives
1 large cucumber, peeled, seeded
  and diced

1 teaspoon dill
3 tablespoons chopped parsley
salt and pepper
cayenne

1. Mix the buttermilk with the chives and let stand for ½ hour.
2. Combine the cucumber, dill and parsley.
3. After ½ hour combine all ingredients.
4. Salt and pepper to taste.
5. Sprinkle with cayenne.
6. Chill for several hours.

Serves 6-8.

Greek Lemon Soup

5 cups (1.2 liters) chicken stock
½ cup (105 g) uncooked rice.
3 eggs
juice of one lemon
salt and white pepper

1. Heat the chicken stock in a saucepan.
2. Add rice, cover and simmer until rice is cooked.
3. In a bowl, beat eggs and lemon juice together. Add ½ cup hot stock, one tablespoon at a time, to the egg and lemon mixture, stirring constantly. Pour into chicken stock.
4. Season to taste with salt and white pepper.

Serves 4.

Cream of Vegetable Soup

2 lb (1 kg) diced vegetables (carrots, onions, celery, leeks, cabbage, turnips, tomatoes)
3 tablespoons (60 g) butter or margarine
5 cups (1.2 liters) beef stock

salt and pepper
4 tablespoons (60 g) barley
2 tablespoons (30 g) cornstarch
milk
2 cups (500 ml) cream

1. Saute the vegetables in the butter in a large saucepan for 10 minutes.
2. Add the stock and bring to a boil. Add salt and pepper. Simmer for one hour.
3. Sieve the vegetables or purée in an electric blender. Return to the saucepan, add barley and continue cooking.
4. Blend the cornstarch with a little milk and slowly add to the soup, stirring constantly. Cook for a further 15-20 minutes.
5. Slowly add the cream and heat through but do not boil.

Serves 6-8.

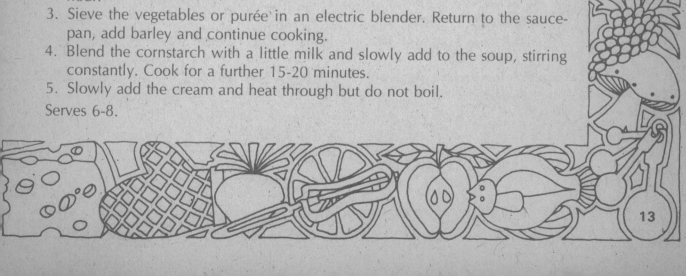

Potato Soup

5 medium potatoes, diced	salt
4 leeks, chopped, white part only	2 cups (500 ml) milk, scalded
2 tablespoons minced parsley	white pepper
2 tablespoons (40 g) butter	2 egg yolks
or margarine	croutons

1. Melt butter or margarine in a saucepan and saute the leeks and the parsley until lightly browned.
2. In a large saucepan, place diced potatoes, sauteed leeks and parsley and enough boiling water to cover. Bring to a boil.
3. Add salt. Reduce heat, cover and simmer until potatoes are cooked.
4. Put entire mixture through a sieve or purée in an electric blender.
5. Return to a saucepan and add milk. Heat thoroughly.
6. Correct seasoning.
7. Beat in egg yolks.
8. Serve with a teaspoon of butter and a few croutons in each bowl.

Serves 4-6.

Pork and Cabbage Soup

2 tablespoons soy sauce	½ cabbage, shredded
2 egg yolks	6 peppercorns
1½ lb (750 g) ground pork	salt and pepper
1 teaspoon salt	1 egg plus 2 egg whites, beaten
5 cups (1.2 liters) chicken stock	

1. Combine soy sauce, egg yolks, minced pork and salt.
2. Roll into small balls and bring to a boil in the chicken stock.
3. Simmer for 15 minutes.
4. Add the cabbage and peppercorns. Season with salt and pepper and cook for five minutes.
5. Add the beaten egg and stir well. Cook for two minutes and serve immediately.

Serves 6.

Tomato Soup with Salmon

1 large onion, chopped	½ teaspoon crushed thyme
½ green pepper, chopped	1½ teaspoons salt
½ cup chopped celery	¼ teaspoon pepper
2 tablespoons (40 g) butter	2 chicken stock cubes
or margarine	1 lb (500 g) tomatoes
3 cups diced potatoes	1 large can salmon
4 cups (1 liter) water	2 tablespoons sherry

1. Melt the butter or margarine in a saucepan and saute the onion, green pepper and celery for five minutes.
2. Add all the ingredients, except the salmon and sherry, and simmer for about 15 minutes.
3. Add salmon, broken into chunks, and the liquid from the can. Mix well
4. Add sherry and heat through.

Serves 4-6.

Beer and Milk Soup

1 bottle (26 oz) beer	2 egg yolks
juice of one lemon	sugar and salt
one cinnamon stick	croutons of fried bread
2½ cups (625 ml) milk	

1. Heat the beer in a saucepan with the lemon juice and cinnamon.
2. In a separate saucepan, heat the milk and pour it over the beaten egg yolks, stirring constantly whilst pouring.
3. Add the milk and egg mixture to the hot beer. Season to taste with salt and sugar. Heat thoroughly but do not boil.
4. Serve topped with the croutons.

Serves 4.

Cream of Chicken Soup with Herbs

1 medium chicken, cut up
4 cups (1 liter) chicken stock
1 bay leaf
1 onion, chopped
1 stalk celery, chopped
1 carrot, sliced
½ cup (125 g) butter
  or margarine
½ cup (62.5 g) flour
2 cups (500 ml) milk
2 cups (500 ml) cream
¼ teaspoon each dried thyme,
  marjoram and chives (or
  fresh herbs)
⅛ teaspoon nutmeg
½ teaspoon turmeric
¾ cup cooked rice
salt and pepper
chopped parsley
toasted sesame seeds

1. Put chicken, chicken stock, bay leaf, onion, celery and carrot into a large saucepan and bring to a boil. Reduce heat, cover and simmer for 1½ hours or until chicken is tender.
2. Remove skin and bones from chicken and cut meat into bite-size pieces.
3. Strain broth and put aside.
4. Melt butter or margarine in a large saucepan and blend in flour.
5. Add milk and cream and cook gently until thickened, stirring constantly.
6. Add herbs, nutmeg, turmeric, rice, chicken broth and chicken. Heat thoroughly but do not boil.
7. Season to taste with salt and pepper. Garnish with parsley and sesame seeds.

Serves 8.

Anchovy and Rice Soup

¼ cup (62.5 g) butter
or margarine
1 large onion, minced
3 tablespoons minced parsley
½ cup (105 g) uncooked rice

1 can anchovy fillets, mashed
3 cans beef consomme
3 cans water
grated Parmesan cheese

1. Melt butter or margarine in a saucepan. Add onion and parsley and saute for five minutes.
2. Add remaining ingredients, except cheese. Cover and simmer for 30 minutes.
3. Garnish with cheese.

Serves 4-6.

Fish Soup

1 lb (500 g) white fish
1 tablespoon (20 g) butter
or margarine
1 large onion, chopped
3 stalks celery, diced

2 large tomatoes, chopped
6 cups (1.2 liters) water
1 teaspoon salt
½ teaspoon thyme

1. Cut fish into bite-size pieces.
2. In a large saucepan, saute onions, celery and tomatoes in butter for three minutes.
3. Add fish and water, salt and thyme and cook, covered, over low heat for ½ hour.

Serves 4-6.

17

Chicken Soup with Swedish Dumplings

6 cups (1.5 litres) chicken stock
2 cups diced cooked chicken
½ cup chopped celery
4 tablespoons flour
1 cup (250 ml) milk
1 teaspoon salt
2 cardamon seeds, crushed
or ¼ teaspoon nutmeg

1 tablespoon sugar
2 tablespoons (40 g) butter
or margarine
1 egg
8 blanched almonds, chopped finely
2 tablespoons fresh parsley,
minced

1. Bring stock, chicken and celery to a boil in a large saucepan.
2. Make dumplings in a separate saucepan by blending flour and a little milk to make a paste. Add remaining milk, salt, cardamon and sugar. Cook until thickened, stirring constantly. Add butter and stir until melted. Remove from heat. Add egg, mix well and cool. Add almonds and parsley.
3. Drop the dumpling mixture by the tablespoon into the boiling soup.
4. Cook for two minutes or until dumplings rise to the top.

Serves 4-6.

Scallop and Egg Soup

1 lb (500 g) fresh scallops
5 cups (1.2 liters) chicken
stock
salt and pepper

4 eggs, beaten
3 scallions, chopped (green and
white parts)

1. Cut up scallops and add to the chicken stock in a large saucepan.
2. Season with salt and pepper and bring to a boil. Reduce heat and simmer for ½ hour.
3. Stir in eggs and scallions. Simmer for three minutes.
4. Add more salt and pepper if desired.

Serves 4.

Peanut Butter Soup (1)

½ lb (250 g) beef
  or lamb, cubed
1 medium onion, chopped
1 teaspoon salt
6 cups (1.5 liters) water
2 cups (530 g) peanut butter

1 green pepper, chopped
2 tomatoes, chopped
½ lb (250 g) eggplant, chopped
½ lb (250 g) smoked fish
small can crabmeat, optional

1. In a large saucepan combine half the onion with the meat, salt and water. Bring to a boil, reduce heat and simmer until meat is tender.
2. Mix peanut butter with a little water and cook mixture (in a separate saucepan) stirring constantly, until it thickens and oil collects on the surface. Add to the meat and water.
3. Add pepper, tomatoes, eggplant and other half of the onion and cook for 20 minutes. Stir occasionally.
4. Add fish and crabmeat to the soup and simmer for another 15 minutes.

Serves 6.

Peanut Butter Soup (2)

1 chicken, cut up into small
  pieces
1 teaspoon salt
½ teaspoon black pepper
6 cups (1.5 liters) water

1 green pepper, chopped
2 onions, chopped
4 tablespoons (80 g) peanut
  butter
1 tablespoon tomato paste

1. Season chicken with salt and pepper and let stand for 10 minutes.
2. In a large saucepan, combine water, green pepper, onions and bring to a boil.
3. Add chicken and peanut butter. Reduce heat and cook partially covered for about one hour, stirring occasionally.
4. Skim off fat.
5. Add tomato paste and stir well.
6. Season to taste and cook for another ten minutes.

Serves 6.

Portuguese Egg Soup

2 large onions, sliced	½ teaspoon thyme
1 clove garlic, crushed	1 teaspoon salt
½ cup finely chopped celery	¼ teaspoon pepper
1 tablespoon olive or vegetable oil	4 eggs
6 cups (1.5 liters) chicken stock	minced parsley

1. In a large saucepan saute the onions, garlic and celery in the oil for five minutes.
2. Add stock and seasoning and bring to a boil. Reduce heat and simmer for five minutes.
3. Drop eggs one at a time into simmering broth and poach for five minutes.
4. Remove eggs putting one in each bowl.
5. Fill the bowl with the broth.
6. Garnish with parsley.

Serves 4.

Avocado Soup

2 avocados	2 tablespoons chopped onion
2 teaspoons lemon juice	2 cups (500 ml) milk
½ teaspoon salt	1 cup (250 ml) cream
¼ teaspoon paprika	1 cup (250 ml) chicken stock

1. Mash avocados through a sieve. Put in top of double boiler.
2. Add lemon juice, salt, paprika, onion and mix well.
3. Place top over simmering water. Add milk, cream and chicken broth and stir well. Continue stirring until soup is hot. Serve immediately.

Serves 4.

Special Lamb Soup

3 lb (1.5 kg) stewing lamb,
  cut up
1 medium onion, sliced
1 carrot, diced
½ cup diced celery
salt
¼ teaspoon cayenne

10 cups (2.4 liters) water
¼ cup (62.5 g) butter
  or margarine
3 egg yolks, beaten
juice of 1 large lemon
paprika
spirals of lemon peel

1. Place lamb, carrot, salt, cayenne and water in a large saucepan and bring to a boil. Reduce heat and simmer, covered, for 2-3 hours or until lamb is tender.
2. Skim off excess fat.
3. In a small saucepan, melt the butter or margarine and blend in the flour. Stir in some of the broth and mix well. Add to soup. Blend thoroughly.
4. Season to taste with salt and pepper.
5. Mix egg yolks and lemon juice in a small bowl. Stir in some of the soup.
6. Slowly add egg yolk mixture to the soup, stirring constantly. Heat through but do not boil.
7. Garnish with paprika and lemon peel.

Serves 8-10.

Hollandaise Soup

1 tablespoon each chopped carrot and green peas to garnish	2½ cups (600 ml) chicken stock
	salt and pepper
2 tablespoons (40 g) butter or margarine	1 cup (250 ml) milk
	1 egg yolk
4 tablespoons plain flour	2-3 tablespoons cream

1. Make the garnish by cooking carrots and green peas in a little boiling salted water. Drain and reserve.
2. Melt the butter in a thick-bottomed saucepan. Remove from heat, add the flour and mix thoroughly.
3. Return the saucepan to the heat and cook but do not brown.
4. Slowly add the stock seasoned with salt and pepper, stirring constantly, and bring to a boil.
5. Add half the milk and mix well.
6. Blend the egg yolk, cream and remaining milk and slowly add to the soup, stirring constantly, until soup thickens. Do not boil.
7. Garnish with carrots and peas.

Serves 4.

Kidney Soup

2 tablespoons (40 g) butter or margarine	½ lb (250 g) kidneys
	5 cups (1.2 liters) beef stock
1 onion, chopped	salt, pepper and thyme
2 stalks celery, chopped	4 tablespoons cornstarch
1 carrot, diced	½ cup (125 ml) milk

1. Melt the butter in a large saucepan and saute the vegetables.
2. Add the chopped kidneys, the stock and the seasonings. Bring to a boil. Reduce heat and simmer for 2-2½ hours.
3. Add the blended cornstarch and milk to the soup, stirring constantly.
4. Simmer for another 15 minutes.

Serves 4.

Bacon and Bean Soup

1 cup (200 g) dried beans	1 cup diced potatoes
4 cups (1 liter) water	1 cup diced celery
½ lb (250 g) bacon	2 large tomatoes, cut up
1 onion, chopped	2 tablespoons flour
2 teaspoons salt	2 cups (500 ml) warm milk
¼ teaspoon pepper	

1. Put beans and water in a large saucepan. Bring to a boil and boil for five minutes.
2. Remove from heat and let stand for one hour.
3. Cut bacon into small pieces and saute with onions until lightly browned.
4. Add, along with the fat, to the beans. Cover and simmer for one hour.
5. Add the remaining ingredients except for the flour and milk and simmer for ½ hour.
6. Mix the flour with a little cold water and stirring constantly, add to the beans.
7. Just before serving add warm milk and blend thoroughly.

Serves 6.

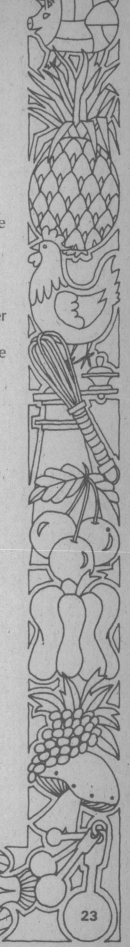

Mulligatawny

1 chicken, cut into pieces
6 cups (1.5 liters) water
salt
3 medium onions, quartered
1 stalk celery, chopped
3 carrots, chopped
1 clove garlic, crushed
1 green apple, chopped
¼ cup vegetable oil
½ cup flour
curry powder to taste
pinch cayenne
pepper
hot cooked rice
chopped parsley

1. Put chicken in a large saucepan with water, 2 teaspoons salt, 2 of the 3 onions, celery and carrots. Bring to a boil. Reduce heat, cover and simmer for ½ hour.
2. Chop the remaining onion and saute with the garlic and apple in the oil for five minutes.
3. Blend in the flour and curry powder.
4. Add one cup broth from the chicken and simmer for ten minutes longer.
5. Slowly pour into the large saucepan with the chicken, mix thoroughly and simmer for ½ hour.
6. Add cayenne, salt and pepper to taste.
7. Put a serving of rice in each soup bowl, pour soup over it and garnish with parsley.

Serves 6-8.

Cabbage Soup

2 lb (1 kg) chuck steak
   in one piece
2 lb (1 kg) beef soup bones
8 cups (2 liters) water
1 tablespoon salt
¼ teaspoon pepper
1 large can tomatoes

1 onion, chopped
1 clove garlic, crushed
2 tablespoons chopped parsley
1 small cabbage
1 tablespoon sugar
1 tablespoon vinegar
minced fresh dill or dill seeds

1. Put all ingredients, except last four, in a large saucepan. Bring to a boil. Reduce heat, cover and simmer for 1½ hours.
2. Cut up cabbage coarsely and with the sugar and vinegar, add to soup.
3. Simmer for another 1½ hours or until meat is tender. Skim off fat.
4. Remove meat and cut it into bite-size pieces. Discard bones.
5. Correct seasoning.
6. Garnish with dill.

Serves 8-10.

Cheese Soup

½ cup (125 g) butter
   or margarine
2 onions, chopped
2 cloves garlic, crushed
2 stalks celery, chopped
   (including leaves)

1 lb (500 g) sharp cheddar
   cheese, grated
½ cup flour
1 cup white wine
5 cups (1.2 liters) milk
salt and pepper

1. Melt butter in a large saucepan and saute the onions, garlic and celery for five minutes.
2. Add flour and blend well.
3. Over very low heat, add cheese, wine and milk, stirring constantly.
4. Heat thoroughly but do not boil.

Serves 4-6.

Pepper Pot Soup

veal bone
1 lb (500 g) stewing veal, cut
 into bite-size pieces
½ lb (250 g) tripe, cubed
1 bay leaf
salt
10 whole black peppercorns
3 onions, diced
6 cups (1.5 liters) water

2 potatoes, diced
2 carrots, diced
¼ cup diced celery
½ medium green pepper, chopped
2 tablespoons (40 g) butter
 or margarine
pepper
minced parsley

1. Put bone, veal, tripe, bay leaf, 2 teaspoons salt, whole peppercorns and one-third of the onions in a large saucepan. Add water and mix thoroughly.
2. Bring to a boil. Reduce heat, cover and simmer for two hours. Remove bone.
3. Cook remaining onion, potatoes, carrots, celery and green pepper in butter in another saucepan for ten minutes.
4. Add to the meat mixture and simmer for ½ hour.
5. Season to taste with salt and pepper.
6. Garnish with parsley.

Serves 6-8.

Lobster Bisque

2 tablespoons small seed tapioca
1½ teaspoons salt
¼ teaspoon pepper
¼ teaspoon paprika
1 tablespoon minced onion
3 cups (750 ml) milk

1 cup (250 ml) cream
1½ cups cooked lobster meat
2 tablespoons (40 g) butter
   or margarine
2 tablespoons sherry
   or brandy

1. In the top of a double boiler mix tapioca, salt, pepper, paprika, onion, milk and cream.
2. Put over rapidly boiling water and cook for fifteen minutes or until tapioca is soft. Stir constantly.
3. Add lobster and butter. Blend well.
4. Reduce heat until water is simmering.
5. When lobster is heated through, add sherry or brandy and serve immediately.

Serves 4.

Chicken and Almond Soup

2 tablespoons olive or vegetable oil
½ lb (250 g) cooked chicken,
   cut into bite-size pieces
1½ cups (175 g) almonds,
   finely chopped
½ onion, chopped

2 cloves garlic, crushed
2 tablespoons chopped parsley
¼ cup (30 g) bread crumbs
5 cups (1.2 liters) chicken stock
salt and pepper

1. Heat the oil in a large saucepan. Add the chicken, almonds, onion, garlic and half the parsley. Saute until the onions are transparent.
2. Add the bread crumbs and cook for three minutes.
3. Add the stock, mix well and season to taste with salt and pepper.
4. Simmer for ½ hour.
5. Garnish with remaining parsley.

Serves 4.

27

Cockaleekie Soup

salt
1 boiled chicken, cut into pieces
9 cups (2½ liters) water
3 onions, sliced
1 clove garlic, crushed
1 tablespoon chopped parsley
1 bay leaf

1 teaspoon poultry seasoning
dash cayenne
12 leeks, sliced
   (white part only)
6 medium potatoes, peeled and diced
pepper

1. Put one tablespoon salt and all ingredients except last three in a large saucepan. Bring to a boil. Reduce heat and simmer, covered, for 3 hours or until chicken is tender.
2. Remove skin and bones from chicken and cut meat into bite-size pieces.
3. Skim fat from broth and add chicken, leeks and potatoes.
4. Cover and cook for ½ hour or until potatoes are cooked.
5. Salt and pepper to taste.

Serves 8-10.

Orange-Tomato Soup

5 cups (1.2 liters) tomato
   juice
2 tablespoons brown sugar
1 onion, chopped
½ cup (125 ml) concentrated orange
   juice

2 tablespoons lemon juice
salt and pepper
1 tablespoon grated lemon peel

1. Combine tomato juice, sugar, onion and orange juice in a large saucepan.
2. Bring to a boil. Reduce heat and simmer for five minutes.
3. Garnish with grated lemon peel.

(May also be served chilled.)

Serves 4.

Vichyssoise

3 tablespoons (60 g) butter
4 leeks, chopped (white part only)
1 small onion, chopped
4 medium potatoes, diced

2½ cups (625 ml) chicken stock
1 bay leaf
1 teaspoon salt
2½ cups (625 ml) cream
chives, minced

1. Melt the butter in a saucepan and saute the leeks and the onion until transparent.
2. Add the potatoes and chicken stock to the saucepan with the salt. Stir and bring to a boil. Reduce heat and simmer until potatoes are soft.
3. Remove the vegetables and put them through a sieve or purée them in an electric blender.
4. Return the puréed vegetables to the soup, let it cool and then chill for several hours in the refrigerator.
5. Before serving add the cream.
6. Garnish with chopped chives.

Serves 4-6.

Cream of Spinach Soup

1½ lb (750 g) spinach, cooked
2 tablespoons (40 g) butter
  or margarine
4 tablespoons plain flour
2½ cups (625 ml) chicken stock

1¼ cups (300 ml) milk
salt and pepper
1¼ cups (300 ml) cream
butter to garnish

1. Sieve cooked spinach or purée in an electric blender.
2. In a large saucepan, blend flour and butter. Slowly add stock and milk. Bring to a boil, stirring constantly. Reduce heat.
3. Add spinach and season to taste with salt and pepper.
4. Stir in the cream and reheat but do not boil.
5. Put knob of butter on top of each serving.

Serves 4-6.

Avocado-Mushroom Soup

1 small onion, minced
¼ lb (125 g) mushrooms, thinly sliced
2 tablespoons minced celery leaves
2 tablespoons (40 g) butter or margarine
2 tablespoons flour

2 cups (500 ml) chicken stock
1 cup (250 ml) milk
1 cup (250 ml) cream
1 avocado, mashed to a paste
salt and white pepper

1. Saute onion, mushrooms and celery leaves in butter or margarine for three minutes or until onions are soft.
2. Stir in flour and blend well.
3. Slowly add milk, cream and chicken, stirring constantly.
4. Bring to a boil. Reduce heat and, stirring constantly, simmer for 4 minutes.
5. Before serving add avocado, blending well; bring to a boiling point again.
6. Remove from heat. Season to taste with salt and pepper.

Serves 4.

Polish Borscht

1½ lbs (750 g) chuck steak, cut into bite-size pieces
5 cups (1.2 liters) water
4 medium beets, cooked and sliced
2 stalks celery, diced

1 onion, minced
salt and pepper
½ cup (125 g) sour cream
2 tablespoons flour
1 egg

1. Put meat and water in a large saucepan and bring to a boil. Reduce heat and simmer, covered, for two hours or until meat is almost tender.
2. Add beets, celery and onion. Cook about 30 minutes longer.
3. Add salt and pepper to taste.
4. Blend together sour cream, flour and egg.
5. Stir into the soup. Heat thoroughly but do not boil.

Serves 4-6.

Curried Cauliflower Soup

3 tablespoons (60 g) butter
or margarine
½ cauliflower, cut into small
pieces
1 green pepper, chopped
2 medium onions, chopped
1½ teaspoons turmeric

curry powder to taste
2½ cups (625 ml) chicken stock
1½ tablespoons flour
1 cup (250 ml) milk
1 cup (250 g) yoghurt
chopped parsley

1. Heat butter or margarine in a saucepan and saute the cauliflower, green pepper and onions for five minutes.
2. Add turmeric and curry powder and mix well.
3. Add chicken stock. Bring to a boil. Reduce heat and simmer, covered, for 20 minutes.
4. In a small bowl, add flour to a little of the milk. Stir well, then add remaining milk.
5. Add milk and flour mixture to the soup.
6. Simmer for ten minutes, stirring constantly.
7. Stir in yoghurt. Reheat.
8. Serve garnished with parsley.

Serves 4-6.

Iced Tomato Soup

1 16 oz can (475 ml) tomato juice
1 cup (250 ml) cream
2 tablespoons sherry
salt and pepper
2 teaspoons brown sugar
minced parsley

1. Mix all the ingredients together in a bowl.
2. Chill for several hours in the refrigerator.
3. Before serving, garnish with chopped parsley.

Serves 4.

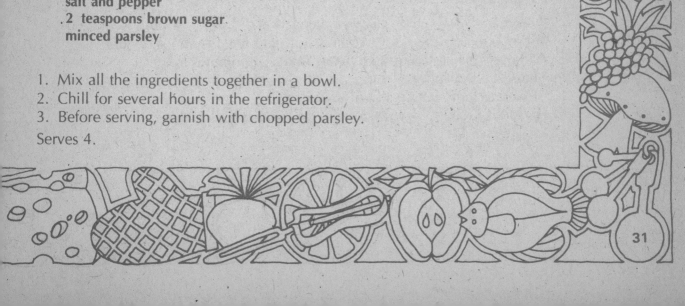

Egg and Lemon Soup

7½ cups (1.8 liters) chicken stock
1 cup (210 g) rice
juice of 2 lemons

3 egg yolks
salt and pepper
chopped parsley

1. In a large saucepan, bring chicken stock to a boil.
2. Slowly add rice and simmer for 15 minutes or until rice is tender.
3. In a small bowl, beat the lemon juice with the egg yolks.
4. Very slowly add a cup of the soup to the egg and lemon mixture, stirring constantly.
5. Pour the mixture into the soup.
6. Bring to a boil. Remove from heat and leave covered for five minutes.
7. Serve garnished with chopped parsley.

Serves 6.

Tomato-Salmon Bisque

1 large can salmon
1½ cups (375 ml) tomato puree
2 tablespoons minced parsley
2½ cups (625 ml) water
1 small onion, chopped

2 tablespoons (40 g) butter
   or margarine
2 tablespoons flour
2 cups (500 ml) cream
salt and pepper

1. Place salmon with liquid from the tin into a large saucepan with the tomato puree, parsley and water.
2. Bring to a boil. Reduce heat and simmer for 20 minutes.
3. In another saucepan, saute onion in the butter or margarine until golden brown.
4. Blend in flour.
5. Remove from heat and add cream, stirring constantly.
6. Slowly pour into salmon mixture. Blend very well.
7. Season to taste with salt and pepper.
8. Stirring constantly, heat thoroughly. Do not allow to boil.

Serves 6.

Lentil Soup with Frankfurters

2 cups (400 g) dried lentils
8 cups (2 liters) beef stock
½ lb (250 g) bacon bones
1 tablespoon (20 g) butter
  or margarine

1 tablespoon flour
3 medium potatoes, diced
2 carrots, diced
1 lb (500 g) frankfurters, sliced
  in ½ inch (10 mm) pieces

1. Cover the lentils with water and soak overnight.
2. Drain and rinse and cover with fresh cold water.
3. Bring to a boil and cook for ten minutes. Drain again.
4. Add the beef stock and the bacon bones and bring to boil. Reduce heat and simmer, covered, for 2-3 hours.
5. Remove bacon bones.
6. Blend the flour and the butter and with the potatoes, carrots and frankfurters add to the soup.
7. Simmer for ½ hour or until the potatoes and carrots are tender.

Serves 8.

Scotch Broth

2 lb (1 kg) stewing lamb, cut
  into bite-size pieces
1 lamb shank
8 cups (2 liters) water
salt
whole peppercorns

½ cup (105 g) barley
1½ cups diced carrots
3 onions, chopped
1½ cups diced celery
thyme
pepper

1. Brown lamb in a large saucepan, stirring often. Pour off fat.
2. Add lamb shank, water, 1 tablespoon salt, a few whole peppercorns and the barley. Bring to a boil.
3. Reduce heat, cover and simmer for about 2 hours.
4. Remove meat, cool and trim off any fat.
5. Remove bones. Return meat to saucepan.
6. Add vegetables, bring to a boil and simmer for ½ hour.
7. Season with thyme, salt and pepper.

Serves 8.

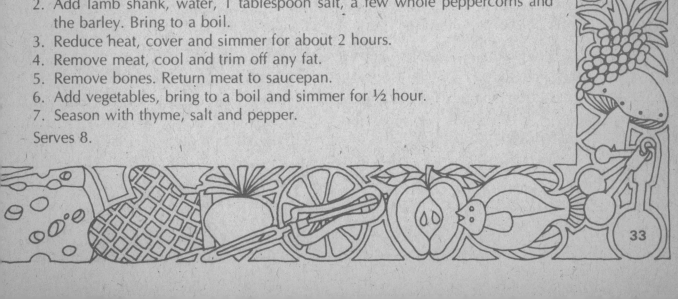

Extra Special Vegetable Soup

2 lb (1 kg) diced vegetables
(carrots, leeks, celery,
cabbage, turnips, etc.)
1 onion, chopped
2 tomatoes
¼ lb (125 g) green beans, cut up
1 clove garlic
2 tablespoons (40 g) butter
or fat

7½ cups (1.8 liters) water
2 tablespoons (30 g) rice
½ cup macaroni
4 medium potatoes, diced
¼ lb (125 g) lean bacon, diced
parsley and basil
salt and pepper
grated cheese

1. Saute all the vegetables in the butter or fat in a large saucepan for 20 minutes over a low heat.
2. Add the water and cook for one hour.
3. Add the rice, macaroni and the potatoes and cook for another 20 minutes or until cooked.
4. Add the bacon and herbs and cook for a further 15 minutes.
5. Season to taste with salt and pepper.
6. Garnish with grated cheese.

Serves 6-8.

Mushroom Bisque

¾ lb (375 g) dried mushrooms
1 lb (500 g) fresh mushrooms,
cleaned and diced
2½ cups (625 ml) water
1 large onion, chopped
3 tablespoons (60 g) butter
or margarine

3 tablespoons flour
2½ cups (625 ml) milk
2½ cups (625 ml) cream
½ cup tomato purée
pinch rosemary
salt and pepper

1. Soak the dried mushrooms overnight. Drain and purée.
2. Cook the puréed mushroom with the water and onion for ½ hour.
3. Brown the fresh mushrooms in butter, add flour and blend.
4. Add milk, cream and tomato purée mixed with a pinch of ground rosemary. Mix well.
5. Combine mixtures. Salt and pepper to taste and cook over a low heat for ten minutes.

Serves 6-8.

Split Pea Soup

2 cups (400 g) split peas
8 cups (2 liters) water
1 lb (500 g) bacon bones
2 medium onions, chopped
1 medium carrot, chopped

1 stalk celery, chopped
3 tablespoons chopped parsley
salt and pepper
2 medium potatoes, peeled and
   sliced raw

1. Cover peas with water and soak overnight. Drain and rinse.
2. Put the peas, 8 cups water, bacon bones, onions, carrot, celery and parsley in a large saucepan. Cover and cook over a low heat for 1½ hours.
3. Season to taste with salt and pepper.
4. Add the potatoes and cook for another 45 minutes or until cooked.
5. Remove the bones and put the soup through a sieve or purée in an electric blender.
6. If soup is too thick, add some boiling water.

Serves 6-8.

Quick Tomato Soup

1½ tablespoons (30 g) butter
   or margarine
4 tablespoons flour
2½ cups (625 ml) chicken stock

2½ cups (625 ml) tomato juice
1 can peeled tomatoes
½ cup (105 g) rice
grated cheese

1. Mix butter and flour in a saucepan.
2. Add chicken stock, stirring constantly.
3. Add tomato juice and canned tomatoes with the liquid.
4. Bring to a boil. Reduce heat and simmer for five minutes.
5. Cook rice in another saucepan. Drain and add to the soup.
6. Garnish with grated cheese.

Serves 4-6.

Black Bean Soup

1½ cups (350 g) dried black beans
ham or beef bones
8 cups (2 liters) beef stock
1 large onion
1 stalk celery, cut in large pieces

1 carrot, diced
4 cloves
1 bay leaf
½ cup tomato purée
salt and pepper

1. Cover the beans with water and soak overnight. Rinse and drain.
2. Put the ham or beef bones in a large saucepan with the beef stock, onion, celery, carrot, cloves and bay leaf. Bring to a boil. Add beans and simmer until beans are soft.
3. Remove bones and bay leaf.
4. Sieve soup or purée in an electric blender.
5. Return to saucepan and add the tomato purée.
6. Season to taste with salt and pepper and reheat.

Serves 6.

Scallop Soup

3 cups (750 ml) milk
1 cup (250 ml) cream
2 tablespoons (40 g) butter
   or margarine
2 tablespoons sugar

1 teaspoon Worcestershire sauce
1½ teaspoons salt
1 lb (500 g) scallops
paprika
chopped parsley

1. In top of double boiler over boiling water, heat milk, cream, butter or margarine, sugar, Worcestershire sauce and salt.
2. Mince scallops and add to the milk mixture.
3. Cook for 5-10 minutes.
4. Garnish with paprika and parsley.

Serves 4.

Bouillabaisse

1 carrot, chopped
3 medium onions, chopped
2 leeks, chopped (white part only)
1 clove garlic, crushed
½ cup (125 ml) olive
  or vegetable oil
3 lb (1.5 kg) white fish, boned
2 large tomatoes, chopped
1 bay leaf

2 cups water
salt
¾ lb (375 g) shelled shrimp
1 dozen oysters
2 pimientos, minced
pinch saffron
½ cup (125 ml) dry white wine
pepper
chopped parsley

1. Saute carrot, onions, leeks and garlic in oil in a large saucepan until golden brown.
2. Add fish cut into bite-size pieces, tomatoes, bay leaf, water and 2 teaspoons salt. Bring to a boil. Reduce heat and simmer for 20 minutes.
3. Add shrimp and oysters and simmer for five more minutes.
4. Add pimientos, saffron, wine and salt and pepper to taste.
5. Garnish with parsley.

Serves 6-8.

Almond Soup

4 tablespoons (80 g) butter
  or margarine
4 tablespoons flour
4 cups (1 liter) chicken stock
1 cup (110 g) ground almonds

1 cup (250 ml) warm milk
salt
paprika
1 teaspoon lemon juice

1. Melt butter in a saucepan. Stir in flour and blend until smooth.
2. Add chicken stock slowly, stirring constantly.
3. Add almonds and cook for three minutes.
4. Add warm milk.
5. Season with salt and paprika. Add lemon juice and serve immediately.

Serves 4.

Minestrone

2 tablespoons olive or
 vegetable oil
2 tablespoons (40 g) butter
 or margarine
1 large onion, minced
2 cloves garlic, crushed
4 tablespoons minced parsley
1 tablespoon tomato paste
8 cups (2 liters) boiling water
2 stalks celery, chopped
2 cups fresh or frozen peas
1 cup shredded cabbage
1 carrot, diced
salt and pepper
½ teaspoon basil
¼ teaspoon oregano
1 cup (150 g) macaroni
1 cup (125 g) grated cheese

1. Heat the oil and butter or margarine in a large saucepan and saute the onion and garlic for five minutes.
2. Add the parsley.
3. Dissolve the tomato paste in one cup of boiling water and add to the saucepan. Cook for five minutes.
4. Add the celery, peas, cabbage and carrot and the remaining boiling water. Cover and cook over a low heat for 45 minutes.
5. Season to taste with salt and pepper. Add basil and oregano.
6. Add the macaroni and cook for 10-15 minutes or until macaroni is tender.
7. Top with grated cheese.

Serves 6-8.

Cucumber Soup, Chinese Style

2 lb (1 kg) soup bones
1 large cucumber, cut into chunks
8 cups (2 liters) boiling water
½ teaspoon sugar
1 tablespoon sherry

1 teaspoon salad oil
1 thin slice ginger
1 lb (500 g) round or flank steak, thinly sliced
salt and pepper
½ lb (250 g) thin noodles, cooked

1. Put soup bones, cucumber and water in a large saucepan and simmer for one hour.
2. In a mixing bowl, combine the remaining ingredients, except noodles.
3. After one hour, add to the soup.
4. Simmer for another 15 minutes.
5. Skim off excess fat.
6. Add noodles and heat thoroughly.

Serves 6-8.

Chestnut Soup

2 onions
1½ tablespoons (30 g) butter or margarine
1 lb (500 g) can unsweetened chestnut purée
5 cups (1.2 liters) chicken stock

salt, pepper and pinch sugar
1 tablespoon cornstarch
milk
2-3 tablespoons cream
2 tablespoons chopped parsley

1. Slice the onions thinly and saute in the butter or margarine.
2. Add the chestnut purée and cook for about five minutes without coloring.
3. Add the stock, seasoning, pinch sugar and bring to a boil.
4. Mix the cornstarch with a little milk and add to the soup.
5. Bring back to the boil. Reduce heat and add the cream. Heat thoroughly but do not boil.
6. Garnish with parsley.

Serves 4-6.

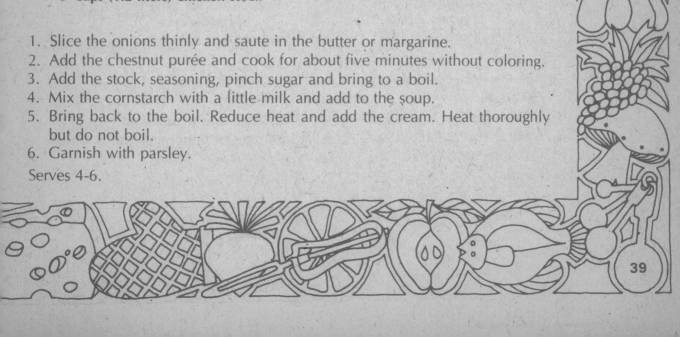

Chicken and Lettuce Soup

1 lb (500 g) chicken breasts
1 teaspoon brown sugar
1 tablespoon soy sauce
1 teaspoon cornstarch
1 tablespoon vegetable oil

½ teaspoon pepper
2 slices fresh ginger
5 cups (1.2 liters) chicken stock
1 lettuce, shredded
salt and pepper

1. Remove chicken meat from the bone and cut into bite-size pieces.
2. Blend the sugar, soy sauce, cornstarch, oil and pepper. Add the chicken and marinate for one hour.
3. Pour a teaspoon of oil in a saucepan and saute the ginger over a low heat for one minute.
4. Add the chicken stock and bring to a boil.
5. Add the lettuce and simmer, covered for five minutes.
6. Add the chicken pieces and simmer gently until chicken is tender.

Serves 6.

Bean Soup

1 lb (500 g) dried beans
  (any variety)
8 cups (2 liters) water
1 cup chopped celery
1 cup diced carrots

4 tablespoons chopped parsley
3 tablespoons tomato paste
½ cup (125 ml) olive
  or vegetable oil
salt and pepper

1. Cover the beans with water and soak overnight.
2. Drain and rinse them in cold water.
3. Put in a large saucepan, cover with the 8 cups of water and bring to a boil. Reduce heat and simmer for two hours or until the beans are tender.
4. When cooked, add remaining ingredients and simmer for ½ hour.

Serves 6-8.

Liver-Ball Soup

2 lb (1 kg) chuck steak,
   trimmed of fat and cubed
2 teaspoons salt
½ teaspoon pepper
1 bay leaf

½ teaspoon oregano
1 cup finely chopped celery
1 lb (500 g) tomatoes, blanched
   and skinned
1 cup carrots, diced finely

1. Cover the meat with cold water, add seasonings and bring to a boil. Reduce heat and simmer for 1 hour.
2. Add vegetables and simmer for 1½ hours.
3. Add liver balls and simmer for 15 - 20 minutes.

Serves 6-8.

Liver balls: Combine ½ lb (250 g) ground beef liver, 1 cup dried bread crumbs, ¼ cup finely chopped parsley, ½ teaspoon celery seed, ¼ teaspoon salt, pinch pepper, 2 tablespoons flour, 1 large egg. Mix well and chill for several hours. Form into small balls.

Apple Curry Soup

2 cans condensed beef consomme
1 large apple, grated
1 small onion, chopped

1 cup (250 ml) cream
salt and pepper
curry powder to taste

1. Cook the consomme, apple and onion together until tender, about 5-10 minutes.
2. Sieve or purée in an electric blender.
3. Stir in the cream and season to taste with salt, pepper and curry.
4. Reheat the soup but do not boil.
5. Garnish with a little grated apple.

Serves 4.

Cheese Soup with Frankfurters

1 onion, diced	2 cups (500 ml) beef stock
1 cup diced celery	1 carrot, diced
¼ cup (62.5 g.) butter or margarine	4 cups (1 liter) milk
¼ cup flour	½ lb (250 g) matured cheese, grated
½ teaspoon dry mustard	salt and pepper
1 teaspoon Worcestershire sauce	3 frankfurters, thinly sliced
½ teaspoon garlic salt	

1. In a large saucepan, saute onion and celery in butter for about five minutes.
2. Blend in flour, mustard, Worcestershire sauce, garlic salt. Stir well.
3. Add beef stock and carrot and bring to a boil. Reduce heat and simmer, covered for 15 minutes.
4. Add milk and heat until almost boiling.
5. Add cheese and stir until cheese is melted.
6. Season to taste with salt and pepper.
7. Add frankfurters and heat through.

Serves 6.

Celery Soup

½ bunch celery	½ cup flour
4 cups (1 liter) water	1 cup (250 ml) cream
1¼ cups (300 ml) milk	salt and pepper
1 onion, sliced	
¼ cup (62.5 g) butter or margarine	

1. Cut up the celery and cook in the water until tender. Sieve or purée in an electric blender. Return to a large saucepan.
2. Place the milk and onion in a small saucepan and bring to a boil.
3. Remove the onion and add the flavored milk to the celery purée.
4. Melt the butter or margarine and add the flour. Blend well.
5. Mix the flour and butter with the cream. Slowly add to the soup.
6. Reheat and season to taste with salt and pepper.

Serves 6.

Chick Pea Soup

1 lb (500 g) dried chick peas	½ lb (250 g) bacon
8 cups (2 liters) water	2 medium onions, chopped
2 lb (1 kg) beef cut into	2 teaspoons salt
small pieces	¼ teaspoon pepper

1. Cover the peas with water and soak them overnight. Drain.
2. Boil the 8 cups of water and add the chick peas. Simmer for ½ hour.
3. Add the beef and cook for another ½ hour.
4. In a small frypan, half cook the bacon. Break it into small pieces and add it to the chick peas and beef.
5. Cover and simmer for another hour.
6. Add the onion and season to taste with the salt and pepper. Cook one more hour.

Serves 6-8.

(For variations, add ½ lb (250 g) spicy sausage or salami cut in cubes before final hour of cooking.)

Oyster Soup

3 dozen small oysters with liquid	4 cups (1 liter) hot milk
½ cup (125 g) butter	4 cups (1 liter) warm cream
or margarine	salt and pepper
¼ teaspoon Worcestershire sauce	paprika
pinch cayenne	

1. Cook oysters, butter, Worcestershire sauce and cayenne in a saucepan until the edges of oysters begin to curl.
2. Add milk and cream.
3. Heat but do not boil.
4. Add salt and pepper to taste.
5. Garnish with paprika.

Serves 6.

Quick Tomato-Celery Soup

1 small onion, chopped
2 tablespoons (40 g) butter
1 can (425 g) condensed
   tomato soup
1 can water

1 tablespoon chopped parsley
½ cup finely chopped celery
1 tablespoon lemon juice
1 teaspoon sugar
salt and pepper

1. Saute onion in butter until golden brown.
2. Add tomato soup, water, parsley, celery, lemon juice and sugar.
3. Bring to a boil. Reduce heat and simmer for five minutes.
4. Add salt and pepper to taste.

Serves 4.

Cold Cucumber Soup

3 onions, chopped
2 tablespoons (40 g) butter
   or margarine
3 cups (750 ml) chicken stock,
   boiling
½ cup chopped parsley
½ cup finely chopped celery

3 medium potatoes, peeled and
   quartered
½ teaspoon thyme
dash Tabasco sauce
2 cups (500 g) sour cream
1 teaspoon salt
1 large cucumber, finely grated

1. Saute onion in butter or margarine for five minutes.
2. Add chicken stock, parsley, celery, potatoes and thyme to the onions and bring to a boil. Reduce heat, cover and simmer for 20 minutes or until the potatoes are tender.
3. Sieve or purée in an electric blender. Cool.
4. Add Tabasco sauce, sour cream and cucumber and mix well.
5. Cover and refrigerate for several hours.

Serves 4-6.

Asparagus Soup

5 cups (1.2 liters) chicken stock
½ lb (250 g) shredded cooked chicken
1 bunch fresh asparagus, cooked and cut up or 1 can asparagus pieces

1 medium onion, chopped
2 scallions, chopped (white and green parts)
salt and pepper

1. Put chicken stock in a large saucepan and bring to a boil.
2. Add chicken and asparagus pieces and simmer for ten minutes.
3. Add onion and scallions and simmer for another ten minutes.
4. Season to taste with salt and pepper.

Serves 4-6.

Avocado Yoghurt Soup

3 avocados, mashed or sieved
2 cups (500 g) plain yoghurt
2 cups (500 ml) beef stock
2 tablespoons grated onion

2 teaspoons chili powder (or to taste)
2 tablespoons lemon juice
1 teaspoon salt

1. Combine all ingredients. Blend well.
2. Season to taste with salt.
3. Chill for several hours before serving.

Serves 4-6.

Lamb Shanks and Rice Soup

4 lamb shanks	2 medium carrots, chopped
2 onions, chopped	3 tablespoons (60 g) butter
1 cup chopped celery	¾ cup (160 g) rice

1. In a large pot, cover lamb shanks with water and bring to a boil.
2. In a frypan, saute onions, celery and carrots in butter for about ten minutes.
3. Add the vegetables to the lamb shanks and boiling water. Bring to a boil. Reduce heat and simmer, covered, for about two hours or until meat is tender. Add more water if necessary.
4. Remove the bones and cut the meat into small pieces. Return the meat to the pot.
5. Add the rice and cook until the rice is tender.
6. Season to taste with salt and pepper.

Serves 6.

Tomato Madrilene

5 cups (1.2 liters) chicken stock	2 bay leaves
1½ lb (750 g) tomatoes, fresh or canned	2 teaspoons salt
1 cup diced celery	½ tablespoon whole peppercorns cayenne
1 onion, chopped	1½ tablespoons lemon juice
4 tablespoons chopped parsley	1 teaspoon sugar
4 cloves	2 tablespoons sherry

1. Mix stock, tomatoes, vegetables, cloves, bay leaves, salt, peppercorns and cayenne in a large saucepan and bring to a boil. Reduce heat and simmer for 30 minutes.
2. Strain and cool.
3. Clarify by straining through a double thickness of cheesecloth over a fine strainer.
4. Reheat, adding lemon juice, sugar and sherry.

Serves 4-6.

Lettuce and Herb Soup

1 lettuce, shredded
6 spring onions, chopped
1 tablespoon fresh mint, chopped
6 tarragon leaves, chopped
1 tablespoon chopped parsley
1 tablespoon chopped chives
½ tablespoon chopped dill
5 cups (1.2 liters) chicken stock
salt and pepper

1. Put chicken stock in a large saucepan and bring to a boil.
2. Add lettuce, onions and herbs, cover and simmer for 15 minutes.
3. Add salt and pepper to taste.

Serves 4-6.

Consomme with Egg Puffs

2 tablespoons (40 g) bacon fat or butter
3 tablespoons flour
water
2 eggs
salt and pepper
1 cup fresh peas, cooked
1 cup finely chopped celery
6 cups (1.5 liters) beef consomme
minced parsley

1. Brown the flour in the bacon fat or butter. Add enough water to make a thick paste.
2. Remove from fire and add the eggs, one at a time, beating after each addition.
3. Season with salt and pepper and cool.
4. In a separate saucepan, add the peas and the celery to the consomme and, when boiling, drop in a teaspoon of the batter at a time.
5. Add minced parsley and serve as soon as the puffs rise to the top.

Serves 6.

Portuguese Bean Soup

1 cup (250 g) dried red
   kidney beans
8 cups (2 liters) water
3 medium onions, sliced
2 cloves garlic, crushed
¼ cup (62.5 g) bacon fat

7 medium potatoes, diced
2 bay leaves
1 teaspoon ground allspice
1 cup (250 g) tomato paste
salt and pepper

1. Put beans and water in pot and bring to a boil. Boil for two minutes.
2. Remove from heat and let stand for one hour.
3. Bring to a boil again. Reduce heat and simmer, covered for 1½ hours or until beans are tender.
4. Saute onions and garlic in bacon fat until onions are golden brown.
5. Add with remaining ingredients, except salt and pepper, to beans.
6. Cover and simmer for 1½ hours.
7. Season to taste with salt and pepper.

Serves 8.

Meatball Soup

1 lb (500 g) ground beef
1 clove garlic, crushed
1 tablespoon parsley, minced
¼ teaspoon marjoram
¼ teaspoon dried basil
¼ teaspoon onion salt
1½ teaspoons salt
pinch pepper

2 eggs
flour
2 beef stock cubes
4 cups (1 liter) water
2 tablespoons tomato paste
1 lb (500 g) tomatoes
1 small bay leaf, crushed
2 tablespoons uncooked rice

1. Mix ground beef, garlic, parsley, marjoram, basil, onion salt, ½ teaspoon salt, pepper and one egg. Shape into small meat balls and roll in flour.
2. Bring stock cubes, water, tomatoes, tomato paste, 1 teaspoon salt and bay leaf to a boil in a large pot.
3. Add meat balls and rice. Cover and simmer for 45 minutes. Just before serving stir in remaining beaten egg.

Serves 4.

Nutty Crab Soup

½ lb (250 g) crab meat
½ cup chopped cashew nuts
½ onion, chopped
1 cup (250 ml) milk
1 cup (250 ml) cream

1 large can condensed cream
 of mushroom soup
3 tablespoons sherry
sour cream for topping

1. Combine crab meat, nuts, onion, milk, cream and mushroom soup.
2. Simmer for five minutes in a saucepan.
3. Remove from heat, add sherry and blend thoroughly.
4. Put a teaspoon of sour cream on top of each serving.

Serves 4.

Cream of Lentil Soup

1 lb (500 g) dried lentils
8 cups (2 liters) water
3 beef stock cubes
1 onion, chopped
1 clove garlic, crushed
1 carrot, chopped

¼ teaspoon dry mustard
½ lb (250 g) salami, cut
 into small cubes
salt and pepper
1 cup (250 ml) cream

1. Rinse lentils. Cover with water and soak overnight in the 8 cups water. Do not drain.
2. Add stock cubes, vegetables and mustard and bring to a boil. Reduce heat, cover, and simmer for 2 hours or until lentils are tender.
3. Add salami, season to taste with salt and pepper and simmer for another ten minutes.
4. Just before serving, add cream.

Serves 6-8.

Mushroom Soup

1 lb (500 g) mushrooms	¼ teaspoon pepper
1 small onion, chopped	4 cups (1 liter) milk
¼ cup (62.5 g) butter or margarine	½ cup (125 ml) chicken stock
¼ cup flour	¼ cup (62.5 ml) sherry
1 teaspoon salt	

1. Chop mushrooms, including stems, and saute with onion in butter or margarine for ten minutes.
2. Blend in flour, salt and pepper.
3. Stirring constantly, add the milk and chicken stock. Cook until thickened.
4. Just before serving, add sherry.

Serves 6.

Bean Sprout Soup

2 tablespoons (40 g) bacon fat	¼ teaspoon paprika
¼ lb (125 g) round steak	1 lb (500 g) fresh bean sprouts (or equivalent canned)
2 medium onions, finely chopped	6 cups (1.5 liters) water
1 clove garlic, crushed	
3 tablespoons soy sauce	

1. Cut meat into thin strips and brown well in the bacon fat with onions and garlic.
2. Add paprika and 1 tablespoon soy sauce and cook for one minute.
3. Add bean sprouts and cook for two minutes over a low fire.
4. Add water and remaining soy sauce and simmer until meat and bean sprouts are tender (approximately 20 minutes).

Serves 6.

Cold Cheese and Tomato Soup

1 can cream of tomato soup
juice of ½ lemon
2 cups (500 ml) milk
1 teaspoon prepared horseradish
pinch cayenne

½ teaspoon salt
¼ teaspoon pepper
½ cup (125 g) cottage cheese
2 scallions, chopped
cucumber slices, unpeeled

1. Put tomato soup in a large bowl.
2. Add lemon juice, milk, horseradish, cayenne, salt and pepper.
3. Beat with rotary beater or electric mixer until thoroughly blended.
4. Add cottage cheese and onion.
5. Mix well and chill for several hours before serving.
6. Garnish with cucumber slices.

Serves 4.

Tuna-Celery Chowder

1 can (184 g) tuna
1 cup chopped celery
1½ cups (375 ml) water
1 small onion, finely chopped

1 can cream of celery soup
¼ teaspoon paprika
½ teaspoon salt

1. Cook celery and onion in water until tender.
2. Add cream of celery soup and stir well.
3. Add drained tuna, paprika and salt. Heat over low fire for 5 minutes.

Serves 4.

Chinese Egg Drop Soup

2 tablespoons cornstarch
6 cups (1.5 liters) chicken stock
2 tablespoons soy sauce
3 tablespoons vinegar
¼ teaspoon pepper
1 cup combined raw vegetables
(carrot, celery, onion, green or
red pepper, mushrooms, whatever you
like)
½ cup cooked chopped meat, fish
or poultry.
3 eggs, beaten

1. Blend cornstarch with small amount of cold stock in a large saucepan.
2. Add the rest of the stock, mixing well, and then remaining ingredients, except eggs. Bring to a boil. Reduce heat and simmer until clear, stirring occasionally.
3. Slowly stir in eggs.
4. Season to taste and serve at once.

Serves 4-6.

Easy Meat Soup

½ lb (250 g) beef or lamb, diced
6 cups (1.5 liters) water
3 carrots, diced
2 potatoes, diced

1 large onion, chopped
½ cup cornmeal (polenta) or wheatmeal
salt and pepper

1. In a large saucepan, cook the meat in the water until tender.
2. Add carrots, potatoes, onion and cornmeal and simmer until vegetables are tender. Add more water if desired.
3. Season to taste with salt and pepper.

Serves 4-6.

Shrimp Soup with Sherry

¾ lb (750 g) fresh
  or frozen peeled shrimp
1 bay leaf
1 carrot, coarsely chopped
1 onion, quartered
3 cups (750 ml) milk
2 tablespoons (40 g) butter
  or margarine
1 cup minced celery

1 onion, minced
1 tablespoon flour
½ teaspoon paprika
¼ teaspoon white pepper
1 teaspoon Worcestershire sauce
1 cup (250 ml) cream
2 tablespoons sherry
minced parsley

1. Cook shrimp in boiling salted water with bay leaf, carrot and quartered onion for five minutes. Drain. Purée shrimp, carrot and onion in an electric blender.
2. Melt butter or margarine in the top of a double boiler over simmering water.
3. Add celery and minced onion: Cook for five minutes.
4. Blend in flour, 1 teaspoon salt, paprika, white pepper and Worcestershire sauce. Add one cup of milk, stirring constantly.
5. Add puréed mixture, the remaining two cups of milk and cream. Stir constantly over boiling water until thickened.
6. Immediately before serving add sherry and garnish with parsley.

Serves 4.

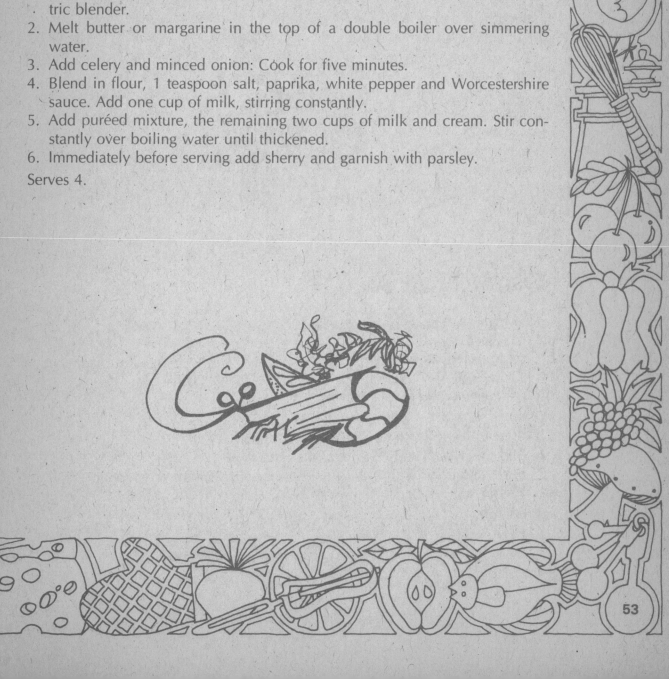

Chinese Mushroom Soup

1 clove garlic, crushed
1 tablespoon vegetable oil
½ lb (250 g) mushrooms, sliced
1 piece root ginger

5 cups (1.2 liters) chicken stock
salt
sesame seed oil or vegetable oil

1. Saute the garlic in the hot oil for a few seconds then remove the garlic.
2. Saute the mushrooms in the same oil for five minutes.
3. Add the ginger and stock and simmer for 1 hour.
4. Remove the ginger, add salt and a few drops of oil. Stir well.

Serves 4.

Quick Oyster Soup

5 cups (1.2 liters) well-seasoned
    chicken stock
12 small oysters
minced parsley
whipped cream or sour cream

1. Bring chicken stock to a boil in a saucepan.
2. Add the oysters and cook until the edges curl.
3. Serve garnished with a little parsley and a teaspoon of whipped cream or sour cream.

Serves 4.

Chicken Soup with Liver Dumplings

½ lb (250 g) chopped liver
1 tablespoon (20 g) butter
   or margarine
1 egg
1 teaspoon salt
½ teaspoon pepper
1 tablespoon chopped parsley

½ cup bread crumbs
6 cups (1.5 liters) chicken stock
½ teaspoon paprika
¼ teaspoon nutmeg
3 tablespoons dry sherry
salt and pepper

1. In a bowl mix the liver, egg and butter together.
2. Blend in the salt, pepper and parsley.
3. Add enough bread crumbs to make a firm mixture.
4. In a large saucepan, heat the chicken stock to the boil. Add the paprika and nutmeg.
5. Drop small balls of liver mixture into the chicken soup and cook until they rise to the top.
6. When all the dumplings are cooked, add the sherry and serve. Season to taste with salt and pepper.

Serves 4.

Beef and Watercress Soup

½ lb (250 g) watercress
½ lb (250 g) lean beef, diced
   finely
1 tablespoon soy sauce
1 teaspoon salt

5 cups (1.2 liters) chicken stock
1 teaspoon sesame seed oil or
   vegetable oil
small can button mushrooms, sliced

1. Wash the watercress and cut off the hard stems. Drain thoroughly.
2. Mix the finely diced beef with the soy sauce, oil and salt in a bowl and leave to marinate for ½ hour.
3. Bring the stock to a boil, add the watercress, stir well and when the soup comes to the boil again, add the oil and meat mixture.
4. Simmer until the meat is cooked — about 30 minutes.
5. Add the mushrooms and simmer for another 10 minutes.

Serves 4.

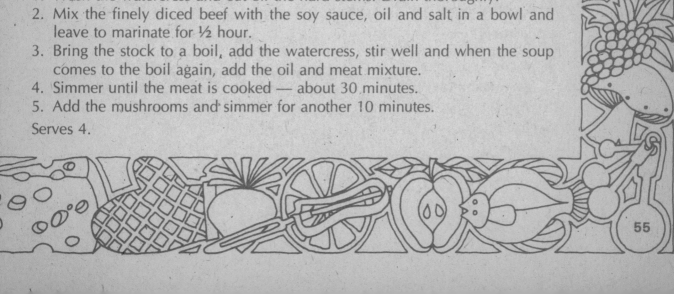

Chicken Meringue Soup

4 cups (1 liter) chicken stock	2 cups (500 ml) hot milk
1 carrot, sliced	2 well-beaten egg yolks
1 small onion, sliced	½ cup (125 ml) cream
1 tablespoon chopped parsley	½ teaspoon salt
2 tablespoons small seed tapioca soaked in ½ cup water	2 egg whites

1. Heat chicken stock, carrot, onion and parsley in top of a double boiler for 15 minutes. Remove and discard vegetables.
2. Add tapioca slowly, stirring constantly, and place over simmering water.
3. Cook until tapioca is transparent, still stirring constantly.
4. Add milk, then egg yolks combined with cream.
5. Continue cooking, stirring constantly, until slightly thick.
6. Season to taste with salt and pepper.
7. Add ½ teaspoon salt to egg whites and beat until stiff.
8. Serve soup in bowls topped with fluff of egg white sprinkled with paprika or chopped parsley.

Serves 6.

Lettuce and Vegetable Soup

2 tablespoons (40 g) butter or margarine	4 tablespoons parsley
1 medium onion, chopped	5 cups (1.2 liters) chicken stock
1 lettuce, shredded	3 egg yolks
½ cucumber, peeled and chopped	1 cup (250 ml) cream
½ lb (250 g) fresh or frozen peas	salt and pepper

1. Melt the butter or margarine in a saucepan and saute the vegetables, lettuce and parsley for 3-5 minutes.
2. Pour boiling chicken stock over the vegetables and simmer for about ½ hour or until vegetables are tender.
3. Beat egg yolks and cream together.
4. Remove saucepan from the heat and slowly add the egg and cream mixture, stirring constantly.
5. Return saucepan to the heat and simmer, stirring constantly, until thickened. Do not boil.
6. Season to taste with salt and pepper.

Serves 6-8.

Chinese Mushroom and Ham Soup

1 tablespoon (20 g) butter
  or margarine
¼ lb (125 g) mushrooms,
  cleaned and chopped
5 cups (1.2 liters) chicken stock
½ lb (250 g) ham, chopped
¼ lb (125 g) bamboo shoots
2 tablespoons white vinegar
1 tablespoon cornstarch
2 tablespoons water
2 eggs, beaten
salt and pepper

1. Saute the mushrooms in the butter or margarine for two minutes. Set aside.
2. Bring stock to a boil and add ham, simmer for two minutes and then add bamboo shoots.
3. Add vinegar, cover and simmer for 30 minutes.
4. Blend cornstarch with the water and slowly add to the soup, stirring constantly. Simmer for two minutes.
5. Add mushrooms and mix well.
6. Remove soup from heat and, stirring constantly, slowly pour in beaten eggs.
7. Reheat soup, if necessary, over very low heat.

Serves 6.

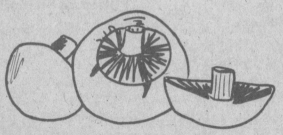

Cauliflower and Ham Soup

2 tablespoons (40 g) butter or margarine
.4 tablespoons flour
7½ cups (1.8 liters) chicken stock
1 small cauliflower, chopped
2 carrots, grated

2 onions, chopped
½ lb (250 g) ham, diced
1 cup (250 ml) cream
1¼ cups (300 ml) milk
3 egg yolks

1. Melt the butter and add the flour. Mix thoroughly and cook for two minutes.
2. Slowly add the stock, stirring constantly and bring to a boil.
3. Add the chopped cauliflower and carrots and blend well.
4. Add the onions and ham and simmer for ten minutes.
5. Season to taste with salt and pepper.
6. Blend cream, milk and egg yolks together in a bowl. Slowly add to the soup.
7. Simmer for five minutes, stirring constantly, but do not boil.

Serves 6.

Pork and Scallop Soup

1 lb (500 g) pork, cut into thin strips
1 tablespoon flour
½ lb (250 g) scallops

7½ cups (1.8 liters) water
1 tablespoon soy sauce
1 teaspoon dried scallions
salt

1. Mix the meat with the flour. Set aside.
2. Cut each scallop into four pieces.
3. Put scallops and water in a large saucepan and bring to a boil. Reduce heat, add soy sauce and scallions and simmer for five minutes.
4. Add pork and flour mixture and simmer for five minutes or until meat is cooked.

Serves 6-8.

Tomato Bisque

2 lb (1 kg) tomatoes, blanched
  and skinned
½ cup (125 ml) water
1 onion, chopped
1 bay leaf
2 cloves
1 stalk celery, chopped
2 tablespoons (40 g) butter
  or margarine
2 tablespoons flour
1½ cups (375 ml) scalded milk
1 teaspoon salt
1 teaspoon sugar
pepper
¼ teaspoon baking soda
1 cup (250 ml) cream
minced parsley

1. Combine tomatoes, water, onion, bay leaf, cloves and celery and simmer for 20 minutes.
2. Remove bay leaf. Sieve the soup or purée in an electric blender.
3. Melt the butter or margarine. Add the flour and gradually add the milk, stirring constantly. Add the seasonings and cook for three minutes.
4. Add the baking soda to the hot puréed vegetables and slowly pour into the white sauce, stirring constantly.
5. Add the cup of cream and heat thoroughly.
6. Add the parsley and serve at once.

Serves 4.

Gazpacho

3 large tomatoes
1 clove garlic
2 tablespoons lemon juice
4 tablespoons chopped parsley
3 tablespoons chopped chives
2½ cups (625 ml) tomato juice
½ cup (125 ml) olive oil

1 green pepper, finely chopped
2 onions, finely chopped
1 large cucumber, peeled, seeded and diced
salt and pepper
dash Tabasco sauce
croutons

1. Combine tomatoes, garlic, lemon juice, parsley, chives, tomato juice and olive oil and purée in an electric blender.
2. Add to green pepper, onions and cucumber. Season to taste with salt, pepper and Tabasco sauce.
3. Chill thoroughly.
4. Serve small bowls of croutons, chives, onions, peppers and cucumbers for garnishing.

Serves 4.

Swiss Gruyere Soup

3 onions, chopped
2 tablespoons (40 g) butter or margarine
4 tablespoons flour
5 cups (1.2 liters) chicken stock

2 cups (250 g) grated Swiss gruyere cheese
salt and pepper
chopped parsley

1. Saute the onion in the butter until golden brown.
2. Add the flour and mix thoroughly.
3. Slowly add the stock, stirring constantly.
4. Bring to a boil. Reduce heat and simmer for 15 minutes.
5. Add the cheese and stir well until melted.
6. Season to taste with salt and pepper.

Serves 4-6.

Borscht

1½ lb (750 g) beets peeled,
    and finely chopped
1 medium onion, finely chopped
juice of two lemons
rind of 1 lemon
2 cups (500 ml) water
4 cups (1 liter) milk

3 eggs
3 egg yolks
Worcestershire sauce
salt and pepper
3 teaspoons sugar
sour cream

1. Boil the beets and onion in the water until cooked.
2. Simmer grated lemon rind and juice in water for a few minutes in a small saucepan and strain into beets.
3. Heat milk. Beat eggs and carefully add to the milk, stirring constantly. Do not boil.
4. Add dash of Worcestershire sauce, sugar, salt and pepper to taste to the egg and milk mixture. Strain and combine with the beets.
5. Chill and serve very cold with a tablespoon of sour cream on each serving.

Serves 6.

Shrimp Soup with Egg

5 cups (1.2 liters) chicken
    stock
3 spring onions, chopped
2 tablespoons sherry
1 teaspoon brown sugar

1 teaspoon soy sauce
½ lb (250 g) peeled
    cooked shrimps
2 eggs
salt and pepper

1. Put chicken stock in a large saucepan and bring to a boil.
2. Add onions and simmer for 15 minutes.
3. Add sherry, sugar, soy sauce and shrimps and simmer for 3 minutes.
4. Beat eggs in a small bowl and add to the soup, stirring briskly while adding.
5. Season with salt and pepper.

Serves 4.

Vegetables and Herb Soup

1 tablespoon (20 g) lard	bunch parsley
2 tablespoons flour	bunch scallions
1 bunch spinach	7½ cups (1.8 liters) water
½ green cabbage	1 teaspoon thyme
bunch beet tops	1 bay leaf
bunch watercress	salt and pepper
bunch radishes	dash Tabasco
2 onions, chopped	¼ lb (125 g) bacon, chopped

1. Wash the vegetables and put in a large saucepan with the water. Bring to a boil. Remove from the heat and drain off the water. Reserve the water.
2. Saute the bacon in the lard.
3. Meanwhile, chop the vegetables.
4. Remove the bacon and saute the vegetables, stirring constantly.
5. When vegetables are well fried, add the flour and season well.
6. Return the bacon and the reserved water to the saucepan and simmer for one hour.
7. Stir in one more tablespoon flour dissolved in cold water and simmer for another ten minutes.

Serves 6-8.

Mushroom and Barley Soup

6 cups (1.5 litres) chicken stock	2 tablespoons (40 g) butter or margarine
1 cup (210 g) barley	2 tablespoons minced parsley
½ lb (250 g) mushrooms	salt and pepper
½ onion, finely chopped	

1. Simmer the barley in 3 cups of chicken stock until soft.
2. Saute the chopped mushroom and onion in butter or margarine for three minutes.
3. Add to the barley with the remaining chicken stock, parsley, salt and pepper.
4. Boil for ten minutes.

Serves 6.

Grape Soup

1 lb (500 g) grapes (seeded and skinned)
2½ cups (625 ml) pineapple juice
1¼ cups (300 ml) water

1 cinnamon stick
2 tablespoons sugar
2 tablespoons small seed tapioca
1 teaspoon grated lemon rind

1. Mix half the pineapple juice and the water in the top of a double boiler. Add the cinnamon and sugar and put over boiling water.
2. Add the tapioca and cook for about 30 minutes, stirring frequently. (Remove the cinnamon stick after five minutes.)
3. Take the saucepan from the heat, stir in the remaining pineapple juice and the lemon rind.
4. Refrigerate for several hours.
5. Just before serving add the seeded grapes to the soup.

Serves 4.

Red Ruby Consomme

4 cups (1 liter) tomato juice
2 cups (500 ml) chicken stock
1 teaspoon chopped chives
1 stalk celery, chopped
½ teaspoon Worcestershire sauce
1 clove garlic, chopped

1 teaspoon sugar
½ teaspoon salt and pepper
2 whole cloves
1 egg white, beaten
1 teaspoon lemon juice

1. Simmer tomato juice, chicken stock, chives, celery, Worcestershire sauce, garlic and seasoning for 45 minutes.
2. Add egg white and lemon juice. Stir well and strain.
3. Serve with toast sprinkled with grated cheese.

Serves 6.

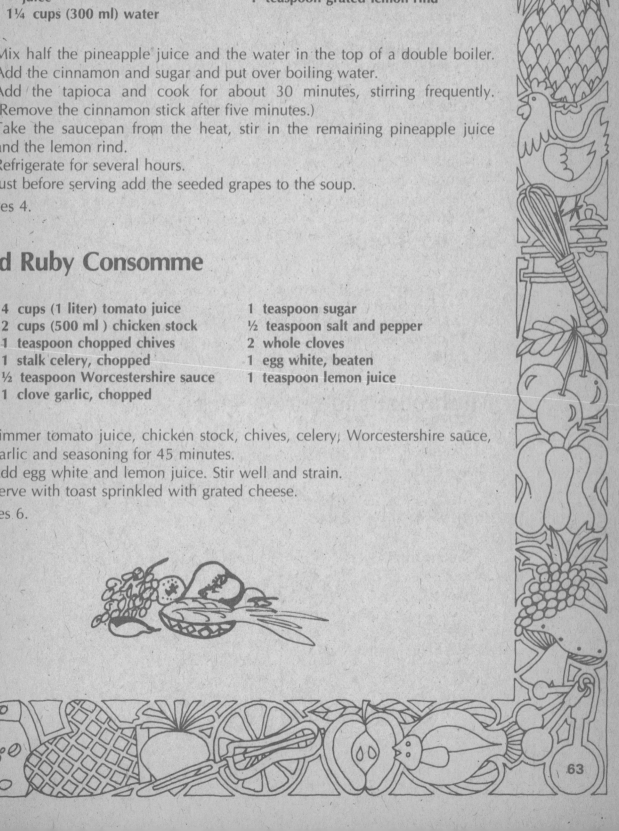

Lentil and Bacon Soup

1 lb (500 g) lentils
5 cups (1.2 liters) water
1 clove garlic, minced
4 tablespoons chopped parsley

salt and pepper
1 lb (500 g) bacon, diced
1½ lb (750 g) potatoes, peeled
and diced

1. Wash the lentils. Cover with the water and soak overnight.
2. Boil them in the same water, with the garlic clove, parsley, salt and pepper.
3. Add the bacon and allow to simmer until the lentils and the bacon are cooked. Add more water if necessary.
4. Add the potatoes and cook for a further 20 minutes or until the potatoes are cooked.

Serves 6.

Salmon Bisque

2 tablespoons (40 g) butter
or margarine
1 onion, chopped
2 tablespoons flour
2 cups (500 ml) cream

1 can salmon
2½ cups (625 ml) water
salt and cayenne pepper
minced parsley
hard-boiled egg, sliced

1. Saute onion in the butter or margarine until golden brown.
2. Stirring constantly, add flour.
3. Add cream and the juice from the salmon. Mix well.
4. Add salmon and water and season to taste with salt and pepper.
5. Simmer for 10-15 minutes, stirring occasionally.
6. Garnish with minced parsley and sliced egg.

Serves 4-6.

Gravy Soup

1 lb (500 g) shin of beef
  or gravy beef
7½ cups (1.8 liters) cold
  beef stock
2 tablespoons (40 g) lard
1 onion, chopped
1 carrot, chopped

1 turnip, chopped
2 cloves
3 tablespoons tomato paste
salt and pepper
2 tablespoons cornstarch
croutons

1. Cut the meat into bite-size pieces and add it to the stock.
2. Melt the lard in a large saucepan and brown the onion.
3. Add the other vegetables and saute lightly.
4. Add stock, meat, cloves, tomato paste, salt and pepper. Mix well.
5. Cover and simmer for 2-3 hours.
6. Blend the cornstarch with a little cold water, stir in and bring to a boil, stirring constantly. Cook for another ten minutes.
7. Serve with croutons.

Serves 6-8.

Chicken Gumbo

1 tablespoon flour
1 tablespoon (20 g) lard
1 onion, chopped
1 medium chicken, cut up
½ lb (250 g) chopped ham
½ red pepper

1 teaspoon thyme
1 tablespoon chopped parsley
1 lb (500 g) tomatoes
7½ cups (1.8 liters) water
1 can okra (optional)

1. Blend the flour and lard in a saucepan and cook until it colors slightly.
2. Add onion and chicken and stir until chicken is browned.
3. Add ham, pepper, thyme, parsley and tomatoes.
4. Add water and bring to a boil.
5. Stir in the okra and simmer for about 3 hours.
6. Remove chicken and cut meat into small pieces. Return chicken to saucepan and simmer for ten minutes longer.

Serves 6-8.

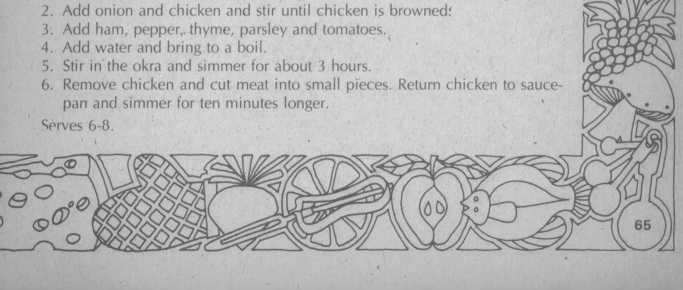

Leeks and Tomato Soup with Meatballs

¾ lb (375 g) leeks
¾ lb (375 g) potatoes
2 tablespoons (40 g) butter or margarine
5 cups (1.2 liters) chicken stock
salt and pepper
1 teaspoon mixed herbs
4 tablespoons flour
1¼ cups (300 ml) milk

1. Wash and slice the leeks and dice the potatoes. Saute them both in the butter or margarine for five minutes.
2. Add the stock, seasonings and herbs and bring to a boil. Reduce heat and simmer for one hour.
3. Sieve the soup or purée in an electric blender.
4. Add the blended flour and milk and bring to a boil. Stir constantly until thick.

Meatballs:

¼ lb (125 g) ground beef
½ onion, grated
2 teaspoons tomato sauce
salt and pepper
¼ teaspoon mixed herbs
1 egg
2 tablespoons flour

1. Mix the meat with the onion, tomato sauce, salt, pepper and herbs.
2. Mix in the egg.
3. Form into small balls and roll in the flour.
4. Add to the thickened soup and simmer for 30 minutes.

Serves 6.

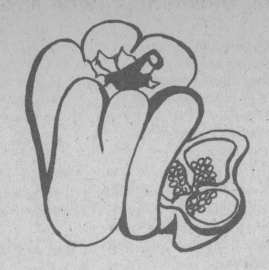

Spiced Cherry Soup

1 lb (500 g) sweet red cherries
rind of ½ lemon
6 whole cloves
3-inch stick cinnamon
½ cup sugar

¼ teaspoon salt
5 cups (1.2 liters) water
3 tablespoons tapioca (small seed)
1¼ cups (300 ml) red wine
thin lemon slices and sour cream

1. Wash the cherries and remove pits and stems.
2. Cover the tapioca with water and set aside for two hours.
3. Remove the rind from the lemon and cut into strips. Stick the cloves in the rind.
4. In a large saucepan, combine the cherries, lemon rind with the cloves, cinnamon, sugar, salt and water.
5. Gradually stir in the tapioca and bring to a boil. Remove from heat.
6. Stir in the wine and allow to cool.
7. Remove and discard the lemon rind, cloves and cinnamon.
8. Refrigerate for several hours.
9. Garnish with lemon slices with a spoonful of sour cream on top.

Serves 4-6.

Potato and Mushroom Soup

2 large potatoes, cubed
1 onion, finely chopped
1 stalk celery, finely chopped
2 tablespoons (40 g) bacon fat,
    butter or margarine
2 tablespoons flour

5 cups (1.2 liters) chicken stock
½ lb (250 g) mushrooms, chopped
salt pepper and celery salt
caraway seeds
1 tablespoon minced parsley

1. Cover the potatoes, onion and celery with water and simmer until tender.
2. In another saucepan, brown the flour in the butter or bacon fat.
3. Add the cooked potatoes, onion and celery with the liquid in which they were cooked to the browned flour.
4. Mix well and pour into the boiling chicken stock.
5. Add the mushrooms, salt, pepper, caraway seeds and a dash of celery salt.
6. Simmer for 30 minutes.
7. Before serving add parsley.

Serves 6.

Poached Egg Soup

5 cups (1.2 liters) chicken
    stock
1 can concentrated
    consomme

8 slices French bread
butter or margarine
4 eggs
grated cheese

1. Heat the stock and consomme in a saucepan and bring to a boil.
2. Saute the bread in butter or margarine in a large frypan until browned on both sides.
3. Poach the eggs in the hot (not boiling) soup.
4. When cooked, place one egg in each soup bowl.
5. Pour the soup over the egg.
6. Sprinkle the sauteed bread with the cheese and serve with the soup.

Serves 4.

Pork and Cucumber Soup

1 large cucumber, peeled, seeded and sliced
½ lb (250 g) pork, cut into very thin slices
1 tablespoon cornstarch
3 tablespoons soy sauce
2 tablespoons sherry
5 cups (1.2 liters) water
1 teaspoon salt

1. Mix thinly sliced pork with the cornstarch.
2. Add soy sauce and sherry to the meat mixture and set aside.
3. Bring water and salt to a boil. Add cucumber and boil for two minutes.
4. Add meat mixture and boil for another five minutes, stirring constantly.

Serves 4.

Pork and Leek Soup

4 oz (125 g) fillet of pork
1 teaspoon salt
1 teaspoon sugar
2 tablespoons sherry
2 teaspoons soy sauce
1 tablespoon cornstarch
2 medium leeks, sliced, white part only
7½ cups (1.8 liters) chicken stock

1. Cut pork into thin slices.
2. Place in a small bowl with the salt, sugar, sherry and soy sauce and mix thoroughly.
3. Add the cornstarch and blend well. Set aside.
4. Bring the stock to a boil in a large saucepan. Add the leeks and simmer for five minutes.
5. Add the pork mixture to the stock. Mix thoroughly and cook for ten minutes.
6. If a thicker soup is desired, blend one teaspoon of cornstarch with a little water and add to the soup, blending well.

Serves 6.

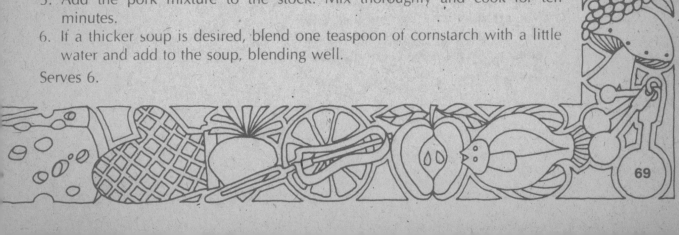

Watercress Soup

2 bunches watercress (about ½ lb or 250 g)	salt and pepper
1 tablespoon (20 g) butter or margarine	1 tablespoon cornstarch
2½ cups (625 ml) chicken stock	1 cup (250 ml) milk
	2-3 tablespoons cream

1. Wash the watercress well and remove the coarse stalks.
2. Melt the butter or margarine in a saucepan, add the watercress (reserving a few sprigs for garnish) and toss over a low heat for a few minutes.
3. Add the stock, salt and pepper. Cover and simmer gently for 20-30 minutes.
4. Sieve or purée in an electric blender.
5. Return to the saucepan, add the cornstarch blended with the milk. Bring to a boil, stirring constantly, and cook for 5-8 minutes.
6. Season to taste with salt and pepper.
7. Just before serving add cream.
8. Garnish with watercress.

Serves 4-6.

Chinese Soup

½ lb (250 g) dried mushrooms	3 tablespoons water
½ lb (250 g) bamboo shoots	1 tablespoon soy sauce
5 cups (1.2 liters) chicken stock	2 tablespoons vinegar
¼ lb (125 g) chopped ham	3 eggs
1 tablespoon cornstarch	salt and pepper

1. Soak the mushrooms for 30 minutes.
2. Chop the mushrooms and bamboo shoots.
3. Bring chicken stock to a boil in a large saucepan. Add the mushrooms, bamboo shoots, ham and simmer for 10 minutes.
4. Add soy sauce, vinegar, cornstarch mixed with the water and cook, stirring constantly for five minutes.
5. Drop in the beaten eggs and stir well.
6. Season to taste with salt and pepper.

Serves 4-6.

Cream of Cauliflower Soup

1 whole cauliflower
2 tablespoons (40 g) butter
   or margarine
4 tablespoons flour
4 cups (1 liter) chicken stock

seasoning and nutmeg
1 cup (250 ml) cream
2 egg yolks, beaten
parsley

1. Divide the cauliflower into small pieces, discarding the green leaves and wash well in salted water.
2. Melt the butter or margarine in a heavy bottomed saucepan, remove from heat and thoroughly stir in the flour.
3. Return the saucepan to the heat and cook for one minute.
4. Gradually stir in the stock, add the cauliflower and bring to a boil. Reduce the heat and simmer for 30 minutes.
5. Sieve the soup or purée in an electric blender, season to taste with salt and pepper and add a pinch of grated nutmeg. Add cream and egg yolks.
6. Reheat the soup and stir constantly until it thickens.
7. Garnish with parsley.

Serves 6.

Tomato Vegetable Soup

5 cups (1.2 liters) water
1 beef soup bone
4 tablespoons chopped parsley
1½ cups chopped celery
1½ cups chopped onion

1½ cups diced carrot
2 potatoes, diced
2 lb (1 kg) tomatoes, cut up
salt and pepper

1. Simmer the soup bone in the water for about ½ hour, covered.
2. Add the parsley, celery, onions, carrots, potatoes, tomatoes and seasonings.
3. Simmer for an hour or until all the vegetables are tender.
4. Adjust the seasoning to taste.

Serves 6.

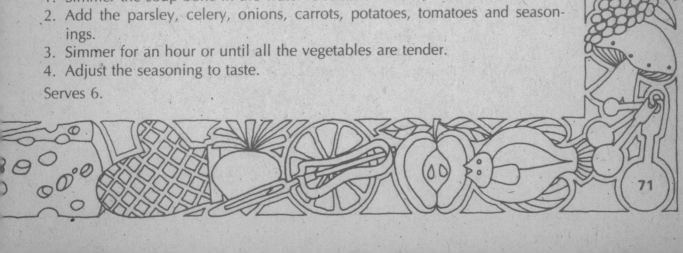

Red Pepper Soup

3-4 red peppers, seeded
5 cups (1.2 liters) beef stock
2 onions, sliced
2 tomatoes, quartered
salt, pepper and cayenne

4 tablespoons cornstarch
pinch sugar
1 strip bacon per person
chopped parsley

1. Simmer the peppers in the stock with the sliced onions and tomatoes until soft.
2. Sieve or purée in an electric blender and season.
3. Mix the cornstarch with a little water and slowly add to the soup, stirring constantly.
4. Reheat and add a little sugar to taste.
5. Roll up bacon, secure with a toothpick and grill for a few minutes.
6. Serve the soup garnished with bacon rolls and parsley.

Serves 4-6.

Quick Pepper Soup

5 cups (1.2 liters) chicken stock
2 tablespoons (40 g) butter
   or margarine
1 stalk celery, chopped

2½ cups tomatoes
2 fresh red peppers, chopped
1 onion, chopped
salt and pepper

1. Saute the vegetables in butter or margarine for five minutes.
2. Add chicken stock and bring to a boil.
3. Reduce heat and simmer for 20-30 minutes.
4. Season to taste with salt and pepper.

Serves 4-6.

Tripe Soup

1 lb (500 g) tripe
7½ cups (1.8 liters) water
1 clove garlic
juice of one lemon

1 egg
salt and pepper
butter
paprika

1. Mince the garlic and boil with the tripe for 2 hours in the 7½ cups water.
2. Remove tripe and mince finely and return to saucepan. Cook ten minutes longer. Season with salt and pepper.
3. In a separate bowl, beat the egg and gradually add the lemon juice.
4. Slowly add a little of the broth from the soup to the egg, stirring constantly to avoid curdling.
5. Add egg mixture to the soup.
6. Garnish with a knob of butter and paprika blended together.

Serves 6.

Lettuce Soup

1 lb (500 g) potatoes, peeled
  and cubed
2½ cups (625 ml) chicken stock
salt and pepper
1 large lettuce

2½ cups (625 ml) milk
2 teaspoons chervil
2 tablespoons (40 g) butter
cream

1. Cook potatoes in the stock until tender. Season with salt and pepper.
2. Wash the lettuce and remove the thick stems. Tear into pieces and add to the potatoes and stock with the milk and chervil.
3. Simmer for 15 minutes.
4. Add the butter.
5. Sieve or purée in an electric blender.
6. Garnish with a teaspoon of cream on top of each serving.

Serves 4-6.

Cream of Pumpkin Soup

2 small onions, chopped
2 tablespoons (40 g) butter
  or margarine
3 lb (1.5 kg) pumpkin
2½ cups (625 ml) water

salt and pepper
3 eggs, beaten
2½ cups (625 ml) milk
grated cheese

1. Cook the pumpkin and put through a sieve or purée in an electric blender.
2. Saute the onion in the butter or margarine until transparent.
3. Put onions into a saucepan with the pumpkin, water and seasonings and simmer for about one hour.
4. Mix the eggs with the milk and add to the soup.
5. Heat the soup very gently for a few minutes to cook the eggs, taking care not to boil or the eggs will curdle.
6. Garnish with grated cheese.

Serves 6.

Tomato Soup

2 lb (1 kg) fresh tomatoes
1 tablespoon cornstarch
2½ cups (625 ml) milk
1 bay leaf
1 clove

6 peppercorns
2 slices of onion
1 tablespoon tomato paste
salt and pepper

1. Cut the tomatoes into quarters.
2. Blend the cornstarch with a little milk. Then add the rest of the milk.
3. Pour into a large pot. Add the tomatoes, bay leaf, clove, peppercorns and finely chopped onion.
4. Bring to the simmering point and simmer until the tomatoes are soft. Sieve or purée in an electric blender.
5. Add the tomato paste. Mix thoroughly.
6. Reheat and season to taste with salt and pepper.

Serves 3-4.

Fish Soup with Brandy

3 tablespoons olive or vegetable oil
2 medium onions, chopped
2 cloves garlic, crushed
½ teaspoon thyme
1 teaspoon saffron
1½ lb (750 g) fish fillets, cut into bite-size pieces

1 teaspoon salt
½ teaspoon pepper
½ teaspoon Tabasco sauce
¼ cup tomato paste
1 cup white wine
5 cups (1.2 liters) water
4 tablespoons brandy
2 cups (500 ml) cream

1. Saute the onions, garlic, thyme and saffron in the oil in a large saucepan until onion is transparent.
2. Add the fish, salt, pepper and Tabasco sauce and cook for five minutes.
3. Stir in the tomato paste, wine and water.
4. Bring to a boil. Reduce heat and simmer, covered, for 20 minutes.
5. Add brandy and cream and simmer for five more minutes.

Serves 6.

Chicken Okra Soup

1 medium chicken, cut up
5 cups (1.2 liters) water
4 onions, chopped
salt and black pepper
¼ teaspoon ginger

2 cloves garlic, crushed
1 tomato, finely chopped
2 red peppers, chopped
1 lb (500 g) canned okra

1. Place chicken in a large saucepan with water, salt, 3 of the 4 onions, black pepper, ginger and garlic. Simmer until meat is tender.
2. Remove chicken from the saucepan and cut meat into bite-size pieces. Discard skin and bones.
3. Return meat to saucepan. Add the tomato and peppers. Boil for five minutes.
4. Add the okra and the remaining onion to the soup and cook for ten minutes longer.

Serves 4-6.

Bean and Almond Soup

½ cup (100 g) dried
beans
3 cups (750 ml) chicken stock
1 cup (160 g) blanched
skinned almonds
2 leeks, finely chopped, white
part only

3 garlic cloves, finely chopped
salt
½ cup (125 ml) white wine
white pepper
1 teaspoon sugar

1. Rinse the beans and cover with cold water. Soak overnight.
2. Drain the beans and cook them in boiling chicken stock until they are almost tender.
3. Crush the almonds. Add the leeks and garlic cloves and mash into a paste with a pinch of salt and the wine.
4. Add the white pepper and sugar. Add the mixture to the soup.
5. Simmer until the beans are very soft.
6. Serve hot or cold garnished with a few whole blanched almonds.

Serves 4.

Avocado Sour Cream Soup

1 large avocado
1 clove garlic
½ cup (125 ml) milk
1½ cups (375 ml) chicken stock
salt and pepper
2½ cups (625 g) sour cream

1. Peel the avocado and cut it into chunks.
2. Sieve or purée the avocado in an electric blender with the garlic, milk, chicken stock and seasoning.
3. Pour into a saucepan and heat but do not boil.
4. Just before serving, stir in the sour cream and gently reheat.

(May also be served chilled.)

Serves 4.

Beef Goulash Soup

2 tablespoons (40 g) butter or margarine	7½ cups (1.8 liters) water
½ lb (250 g) onions, chopped	2 teaspoons salt
1 tablespoon paprika	2½ lb (1¼ kg) potatoes, diced
1½ lb (750 g) beef, cut into bite-size pieces	1 lb (500 g) tomatoes, chopped

1. Saute the onions in butter or margarine until golden brown. Remove from heat and add paprika.
2. Add the meat and replace saucepan on fire. Stirring constantly, fry the meat until most of the juices evaporate.
3. Add 5 cups water and the salt and continue cooking for two hours or until the meat is tender.
4. Add 2½ cups more water and the potatoes and cook until potatoes are tender.
5. Add tomatoes and cook for another ten minutes.

Serves 6-8.

Carrot Soup

1 small potato, sliced	2 tablespoons butter
6-8 medium carrots	*or* margarine
1 medium onion, sliced	4 tablespoons flour
3¾ cups (900 ml) chicken stock	salt and pepper
1¼ cups (300 ml) milk	parsley

1. Simmer the potato, carrot and onion in the stock until soft.
2. Sieve or purée in an electric blender. Add the milk.
3. Melt the butter or margarine in a saucepan, blend in the flour, gradually add the puréed soup and bring to a simmer, stirring constantly.
4. Season to taste with salt and pepper and garnish with parsley.

Serves 4.

Shrimp Soup

3 tablespoons (60 g) butter
  or margarine
2 tablespoons flour
2 tablespoons chopped onion
2 tablespoons chopped celery
¼ cup sliced mushrooms

½ teaspoon salt
¼ teaspoon pepper
2 cups (500 ml) chicken stock
1 cup (250 ml) milk
½ lb (250 g) chopped cooked shrimp

1. Melt butter in a saucepan. Add flour, onion, celery, salt, pepper and mushrooms and cook for two minutes.
2. Add chicken stock and milk gradually, stirring constantly.
3. Cook until thick and smooth.
4. Add shrimp and heat through.

Serves 4.

Mutton Soup

2 tablespoons (40 g) butter
  or margarine
3 medium onions, chopped
1 tablespoon paprika
2 lb (1 kg) mutton, cut
  into small pieces
½ teaspoon caraway seeds

½ bay leaf
5 cups (1.2 liters) water
½ lb (250 g) green peas
½ lb (250 g) potatoes, diced
2 tablespoons flour
1¼ cups (300 g) sour cream

1. Melt the butter or margarine in a large saucepan. Saute the onions until golden brown.
2. Remove the saucepan from the heat and add the paprika, meat, caraway seeds and crushed bay leaf.
3. Add water, mix thoroughly and return saucepan to the fire. Bring to a boil. Reduce heat, cover and simmer for two hours.
4. In a separate saucepan, cook peas and potatoes.
5. When they are cooked, add to the soup.
6. Just before the soup is served, add the sour cream which has been blended with the flour, and simmer for five minutes.

Serves 6.

Fish Chowder

4 cups (1 liter) water
salt and pepper
1 bay leaf
4 whole cloves
1 lb (500 g) white fish fillets
1 tablespoon (20 g) butter
  or margarine

2 onions, chopped
2 tablespoons chopped parsley
3 cups diced potatoes
2½ cups (625 ml) milk

1. Put water, 1 teaspoon salt, ¼ teaspoon pepper, bay leaf and cloves in a large saucepan and bring to a boil.
2. Add fish and simmer for 15 minutes or until fish is cooked.
3. Remove fish and cut into bite-size pieces.
4. In another large saucepan saute the onions and parsley in butter or margarine until the onions are golden brown.
5. Add strained fish liquid and potatoes. Bring to a boil. Reduce heat and simmer, covered for 15 minutes until potatoes are cooked.
6. Add fish pieces and milk. Heat thoroughly.
7. Season to taste with salt and pepper.

Serves 6.

Chicken Broccoli Soup

1 lb (500 g) fresh or frozen
  broccoli (chopped)
1 cup (250 ml) milk
½ teaspoon salt
¼ teaspoon pepper

½ teaspoon dry mustard
1 can (425 g) cream of
  chicken soup
1 cup (250 ml) cream

1. Cook the broccoli in boiling water until tender. Drain.
2. Put broccoli through a sieve or purée in an electric blender. Add the milk, salt, pepper and dry mustard.
3. Add the cream of chicken soup, put in a bowl and chill thoroughly.
4. Just before serving add the cream and mix well.

(If preferred, serve hot. Gently heat the soup but do not boil.)

Serves 4-6.

Catalan Soup

2 strips bacon, chopped
2 small onions, sliced
1 red pepper, chopped
1 stalk celery, chopped
2 large potatoes, peeled and
  thickly sliced
2 large tomatoes, cut in
  large chunks

½ cup (125 ml) white wine
5 cups (1.2 liters) chicken
  stock
¼ teaspoon thyme
1 tablespoon chopped parsley
salt and pepper
2 egg yolks
¼ cup (62.5 ml) milk

1. Saute the bacon and the onions together until the onions are golden brown.
2. Add the pepper, celery, potatoes and tomatoes and mix well. Cook over a medium heat for five minutes.
3. Add the stock, wine, thyme and parsley and simmer, covered, for 45 minutes. Season to taste with salt and pepper.
4. Beat the egg yolks into the milk and slowly add to the soup, stirring constantly. Cook for five minutes being careful not to boil the soup or the eggs may curdle.

Serves 4-6.

Curry Soup

2 tablespoons (40 g) butter
  or margarine
curry powder to taste
4 tablespoons flour

4 cups (1 liter) milk
2 tablespoons boiled rice
salt and pepper
3 tablespoons cream

1. Melt the butter or margarine in a saucepan. Stir in the flour and curry powder and cook for one minute.
2. Slowly stir in the milk. Bring to a boil. Reduce heat and simmer for five minutes.
3. Add the rice to the soup. Season to taste with salt and pepper.
4. Remove saucepan from the heat and stir in the cream. Serve immediately.

Serves 4.

Hot Pot Soup

2 lb (1 kg) beef shin
cold water to cover
½ teaspoon allspice
½ teaspoon peppercorns
½ tablespoon salt
2 cups diced carrots
2 cups diced turnips

1 cup green beans (cut
in one-inch pieces)
½ lb (250 g) tomatoes, chopped
1 onion, chopped
2 tablespoons flour
3 tablespoons cold water

1. Combine beef shin, water, allspice, peppercorns and salt in a large sauce-pan. Cover and simmer for three hours. Remove meat from soup and strain stock.
2. Cut meat from bones and return to stock along with vegetables.
3. Cook until vegetables are tender, about 20 minutes.
4. Mix flour with water until smooth and free of lumps. Stir into soup and cook until slightly thickened.

Serves 8.

Egg Soup

5 cups (1.2 liters) chicken
stock
½ teaspoon meat extract
salt and pepper

2 tablespoons cream
4 egg yolks
1 tablespoon chopped chives
1 tablespoon chopped parsley

1. Heat the stock and add the meat extract. Season to taste with salt and pepper. Remove from heat.
2. Mix the egg yolks with the cream. Stir into the stock.
3. Reheat soup over very low heat. Do not allow to boil or eggs may curdle.
4. Add chives and parsley and mix well.

Serves 6-8.

81

Tomato Beef Soup

½ cup uncooked rice
4 strips bacon, diced
½ lb (250 g) ground beef
2 beef stock cubes

1 tablespoon minced onion
1 lb (500 g) tomatoes, chopped
salt and pepper

1. Cook rice in 2½ cups (625 ml) salted water until tender. Do not drain.
2. Sauté meats together until browned, breaking up beef with a fork. Add to rice with 2 cups (500 ml) water. Mix well.
3. Add stock cubes and onion and bring to a boil. Reduce heat, cover and simmer for 45 minutes.
4. Add tomatoes and simmer for 15 minutes longer.

Serves 4-6.

Tuna-Corn Chowder

1 large can tuna fish
  (packed in oil)
1 large onion, sliced
1 can corn niblets
2 cups diced potatoes

3 cups (750 ml) milk
1 teaspoon salt
2 tablespoons chopped parsley
¼ teaspoon Tabasco sauce

1. Drain tuna. Reserve oil.
2. Add onion to tuna oil in large saucepan and cook until tender, but do not brown.
3. Drain corn and add corn liquid to the saucepan. Bring to a boil and add potatoes. Cover and simmer for ten minutes.
4. Add corn, milk and tuna and mix well. Season to taste with salt.
5. Heat thoroughly. Add parsley and Tabasco.

Serves 6.

Swedish Fruit Soup

2 cups mixed dried fruits
   (apricots, peaches, pears, prunes)
¼ cup seedless raisins
8 cups (2 liters) water
1 cup sugar

one cinnamon stick
3 tablespoons small seed
   tapioca
2 teaspoons Angostura bitters
sour cream

1. Chop dried fruits, place in a large saucepan and pour cold water over them. Allow to soak for one hour.
2. Add sugar and cinnamon and cook slowly, covered, for one hour.
3. Soften tapioca in ½ cup cold water for 15 minutes. Add Angostura bitters and pour into soup.
4. Cook for about ten minutes until soup clears.
5. Cool, then chill thoroughly in refrigerator.
6. Serve in soup bowls with a spoonful of sour cream on top of each serving.

Serves 6.

Potato and Celery Soup

2 cups diced potatoes
1 cup diced celery
3 cups (750 ml) water
3 cups (750 ml) milk
2 cups bread cubes

3 eggs
¼ teaspoon pepper
2 teaspoon salt
1 tablespoon (20 g) butter

1. Cook potatoes and celery in boiling water until tender.
2. Add milk and heat thoroughly.
3. Add bread cubes, then stir well.
4. Add eggs, one at a time, stirring constantly with a fork.
5. Cook over low heat for about 2 minutes, stirring constantly.
6. Add salt, pepper and butter. Blend well.

Serves 4-6.

Potato and Carrot Soup

2 tablespoons (40 g) butter
  or margarine
1 onion, sliced
1 lb (500 g) potatoes, grated
½ lb (250 g) carrots, grated

pinch brown sugar
salt and pepper
4 cups (1 liter) chicken stock
4 tablespoons cream
1 tablespoon chopped parsley

1. Saute the onion in the butter or margarine until golden brown.
2. Add grated potatoes and carrots, sugar and a little salt and pepper. Cook for 5 minutes.
3. Add stock and cook until vegetables are tender.
4. Sieve or purée the potato and carrot mixture in an electric blender.
5. Return to the saucepan and reheat. Season to taste with salt and pepper.
6. Before serving stir in cream and chopped parsley.

Serves 4-6.

Mexican Meatball Soup

½ lb (250 g) ground beef
½ lb (250 g) ground pork
1 egg
1 tablespoon chopped mint
¼ cup fresh bread crumbs
¼ teaspoon pepper

1 teaspoon salt
8 cups (2 liters) beef stock
1 cup (250 ml) tomato purée
1 onion, chopped
1 clove garlic, crushed
chili powder to taste

1. Thoroughly mix beef, pork, egg, mint, bread crumbs, salt and pepper. Form into balls.
2. Combine beef stock, tomato purée, onion, garlic and chili powder. Bring to a boil.
3. Add meatballs, cover and simmer for 45 minutes.

Serves 8.

Egg and Frankfurter Soup

2 cups potatoes, cubed (raw)
2 cups (250 ml) well-flavored
   chicken stock
⅓ cup (83 g) butter
   or margarine
1 onion, chopped
¼ cup flour
5 cups (1.2 liters) milk
1 can corn niblets
¼ teaspoon pepper
1 bay leaf
¼ lb (125 g) Cheddar cheese,
   diced
3 frankfurters, thinly sliced
6 hard-boiled eggs, sliced
salt

1. Simmer potatoes in chicken broth, covered, until just tender (about ten minutes).
2. In a large saucepan, melt butter or margarine over a low heat. Add onion and cook until transparent. Add flour and blend well.
3. Add milk, mix well and increase the heat. Cook, stirring constantly, until mixture is smooth and thick.
4. Add corn (undrained), potatoes with stock, pepper and bay leaf. Bring to a simmer, stirring occasionally. Remove bay leaf.
5. Add cheese, frankfurters and eggs. Season to taste with salt and heat thoroughly.

Serves 6.

Onion Soup

3 large onions, minced	2 cups (500 ml) milk
3 tablespoons (60 g) butter or margarine	salt and pepper
1 tablespoon flour	toasted rounds of bread
2 cups (500 ml) cream	1 cup grated Gruyere cheese

1. In a large saucepan, saute the onions in the butter or margarine for five minutes.
2. Blend in flour. Add cream and milk and bring to a boil. Reduce heat and simmer for ten minutes.
3. Season to taste with salt and pepper.
4. Place toasted rounds in each bowl and pour soup on top. Sprinkle with grated cheese.

Serves 4.

Chicken Soup with Bamboo Shoots

½ lb (250 g) white chicken meat, cut into bite-size pieces	1½ teaspoons fresh grated ginger
1 tablespoon vegetable oil	2 eggs
½ lb (250 g) bamboo shoots, fresh or canned	salt and pepper
5 cups (1.2 liters) chicken stock	2 tablespoons chopped scallions, white and green parts

1. Heat oil and saute the chicken.
2. Add bamboo shoots, chicken stock and ginger.
3. Bring to a boil. Reduce heat and simmer, covered, for ten minutes.
4. Beat eggs and pour into the soup. Simmer for three minutes, stirring constantly.
5. Serve garnished with chopped scallions.

Serves 4-6.

Cucumber and Potato Soup

1. large cucumber, peeled
   and grated
1. lb (500 g) potatoes, chopped
1. onion, chopped
2. tablespoons (40 g) butter
   or margarine
2½ cups (625 ml) chicken stock
½ cup (125 ml) milk
salt and pepper
2. teaspoons chopped chives
1. tablespoon chopped parsley
2. tablespoons chopped mint

1. Melt the butter or margarine in a large saucepan and saute the potatoes and onion for ten minutes.
2. Add boiling stock to the potatoes and onion and simmer until vegetables are tender. Sieve or purée in an electric blender.
3. Return potato purée to the saucepan and stir in the milk and grated cucumber. Season to taste with salt and pepper. Reheat.
4. A few minutes before serving, stir in the chives, parsley and mint.

Serves 4-6.

Fresh Pea Soup

¾ lb (375 g) shelled peas
1 large potato, diced
1 medium onion, chopped
1 lettuce, quartered

2½ cups (625 ml) chicken stock
1½ cups (375 g) yoghurt
juice of half lemon
salt and pepper

1. Put peas, potato, onion and lettuce into the chicken stock and simmer, covered, for 10-15 minutes.
2. Sieve or purée the soup in an electric blender.
3. Return to saucepan and simmer for five minutes.
4. Add yoghurt and lemon juice, blend thoroughly and chill for several hours.

Serves 4.

Claret Soup

1½ cups (375 ml) claret
three-inch piece of cinnamon
1 tablespoon sugar
4 cups (1 liter) beef stock
lemon for garnishing

1. Over a low fire, heat the claret and cinnamon for ten minutes.
2. Add to the beef stock and reheat.
3. Garnish with a thin slice of lemon.

Serves 4.

Jellied consomme

2 cans jellied consomme
juice of 2 lemons
caviar
sour cream
chives, minced

1. Gently mix caviar and lemon juice with the consomme.
2. Top with sour cream and chives.
3. Serve chilled.

Serves 4.

Thick Tomato Soup

1 tablespoon (20 g) butter
 or margarine
1 small onion, chopped
1 carrot, chopped
2 stalks celery, chopped
1 lb (500 g) tomatoes, quartered
1 clove
1 bay leaf

1 teaspoon brown sugar
salt, pepper and paprika
5 cups (1.2 liters) chicken
 stock
4 tablespoons cornstarch
1¼ cups (300 ml) milk
2 tablespoons (30 g) rice
grated Parmesan cheese

1. Melt the butter in a saucepan and saute the onion, carrot and celery for 5 minutes.
2. Add the quartered tomatoes, clove, bay leaf, sugar, salt, pepper, paprika and stock and bring to a boil. Reduce heat and simmer for 1½ hours.
3. Sieve the soup or purée it in an electric blender.
4. Blend the cornstarch with the milk and slowly add to the soup.
5. Bring to a boil again, stirring until thick.
6. Add the rice and simmer gently for ½ hour or until rice is cooked.
7. Garnish with the Parmesan cheese.

Serves 6-8.

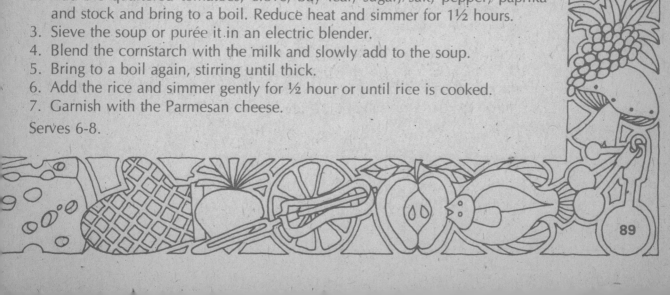

Cherry Soup

2 lb (1 kg) cherries
8 cups (2 liters) water
4 tablespoons cornstarch
2 tablespoons sugar

lemon juice
2 tablespoons red wine
whipped cream or sour cream

1. Wash and pit the cherries.
2. Put cherries in a saucepan with the water and simmer gently for 15 minutes.
3. Sieve the cherries or purée in an electric blender.
4. Return to the saucepan and reheat to the boiling point. Slowly add the cornstarch and sugar mixed with a little water and stirring constantly cook for ten minutes.
5. Add the lemon juice and wine. Mix thoroughly.
6. Chill for several hours.
7. Serve with a spoonful of whipped cream or sour cream on the top of each bowl.

Serves 6.

Chicken Noodle Soup

1 lb (500 g) noodles
5 cups (1.2 liters) chicken stock
1 teaspoon brown sugar
2 teaspoons soy sauce
1 chicken breast, cooked

1. Cook noodles in salted boiling water. Drain.
2. Add chicken stock to the drained noodles with sugar, soy sauce and chicken meat which has been cut into small pieces.
3. Season to taste with salt and pepper.

Serves 4.

Easy Tuna-Tomato Soup

2 cans tomato soup
3 cups (750 ml) chicken stock
1 onion, chopped
1 large can tuna
salt and pepper

1. Blend tomato soup and chicken stock in a saucepan.
2. Add onion and bring to a boil. Reduce heat and simmer for 5 minutes.
3. Add broken up tuna pieces and simmer for ten minutes.
4. Season to taste with salt and pepper.

Serves 4-5.

Chicken-Corn Soup

1 medium chicken
1 onion, quartered
12 cups (3 liters) water
salt
2 stalks celery with leaves,
   chopped

2 cans (425 g each) corn
   niblets, drained
2 hard-cooked eggs, chopped
pepper

1. Put chicken in a large saucepan. Add onion, water and 2 teaspoons salt. Bring to a boil. Reduce heat, cover and simmer for 3 hours or until chicken is tender.
2. Remove chicken from broth and cool. Cut meat into bite-size pieces.
3. Strain broth and skim off most of the fat.
4. Add chicken, celery and corn and simmer for 10-15 minutes.
5. Add eggs and salt and pepper to taste.
6. Simmer for 10 minutes and serve.

Serves 8-10.

91

Basic Stockpot

3 lb (1.5 kg) lean beef
4 carrots
3 leeks
4 medium onions
1 parsnip
3 stalks celery
2 tablespoons chopped parsley

1 teaspoon thyme
1 bay leaf
2 cloves
1 clove garlic, sliced
12 cups (3 liters) water
salt and pepper

1. Put all ingredients in a large saucepan. Do not cut up meat or vegetables; leave whole.
2. Add salt and pepper to taste. Cover and bring mixture to a boil.
3. Reduce heat and simmer for about four hours.
4. Cool the stockpot and remove the fat from the surface.
5. Strain through a fine sieve. Use as a basic stock for other soups or by itself.

Sorrel Soup

½ lb (250 g) sorrel leaves
1 tablespoon (20 g) butter
  or margarine
7 cups (1.2 liters) chicken stock

salt and pepper
1 egg yolk
½ cup (125 ml) cream
2 teaspoons chopped chervil

1. Wash, drain and dry the sorrel.
2. Melt the butter or margarine in a saucepan and cook the sorrel over a low heat for five minutes. Coarsely chop the sorrel and return to the saucepan.
3. Add the chicken stock and seasoning, cover and simmer for 30 minutes.
4. Just before serving add the cream and egg yolk mixed together. Do not allow to boil.
5. Serve garnished with chopped chervil.

Serves 4-6.

Turnip Soup

4 large turnips	1 tablespoon (20 g) butter
2 medium potatoes, cooked	or margarine
4 cups (1 liter) milk	1 teaspoon sugar
2 cups (500 ml) water	salt and pepper

1. Chop the turnips coarsely. Cook them in the water for ten minutes. Drain, reserving the water.
2. Melt the butter or margarine in a saucepan and saute the turnips with the sugar and seasoning for five minutes.
3. Add the coarsely chopped cooked potatoes and the reserved water. Cook until the turnips are very soft. Sieve the mixture or purée in an electric blender.
4. Return the soup to the saucepan and stir in the milk. Reheat if necessary.

Serves 4.

Turkish Soup

1 lb (500 g) tripe, cooked and diced	2 teaspoons salt
6 cups (1.5 liters) chicken stock	3 tablespoons yeast
1 clove garlic, crushed	2 eggs
¼ teaspoon white pepper	juice of one lemon
	juice of one orange

1. Mix together the tripe and the stock in a large saucepan.
2. Add garlic, pepper, salt and yeast and cook over low heat for 15 minutes.
3. Remove from heat.
4. Beat eggs with the lemon and orange juice.
5. Add egg mixture to the soup and reheat.

Serves 4-6.

Mushroom Bouillon

6 cups (1.5 liters) strong
  beef stock
½ lb (250 g) chopped
  mushrooms
1 cup (250 ml) dry sherry
salt and pepper

1. Simmer the mushrooms in the stock until tender.
2. Add salt and pepper to taste.
3. Before serving, add the sherry.

Serves 4-6.

Yoghurt Soup

2 cups (500 g) plain yoghurt
6 cups (1.5 liters) beef stock
1 tablespoon (20 g) butter
  or margarine

1 tablespoon flour
2 tablespoons chopped mint

1. Mix together the yoghurt and beef stock in a large saucepan. Heat but do not boil or soup will curdle.
2. In another saucepan, mix together the butter or margarine and the flour. Cook for 2-3 minutes over a very low heat.
3. Add the yoghurt and stock mixture to the butter and flour, stirring constantly. Heat thoroughly.
4. Serve the soup garnished with the mint.

Serves 6.

Index

Hot Pot Soup 81
Hungarian Soup 12

Iced Tomato Soup 31

Jellied Consomme 89

Kidney Soup 22

Lamb Shanks and Rice Soup 46
Leeks and Tomato Soup with Meatballs 66
Lentil and Bacon Soup 64
Lentil Soup with Frankfurters 33
Lettuce Soup 73
Lettuce and Herb Soup 47
Lettuce and Vegetable Soup 56
Liver-Ball Soup 41
Lobster Bisque 27

Meatball Soup 48
Mexican Meatball Soup 84
Minestrone 38
Mulligatawny 24
Mushroom Soup 50
Mushroom and Barley Soup 62
Mushroom Bisque 34
Mushroom Bouillon 94
Mutton Soup 78

Nutty Crab Soup 49

Onion Soup 86
Orange-Tomato Soup 28
Oyster Soup 43

Peanut Butter Soup (1) 19
Peanut Butter Soup (2) 19
Pepper Pot Soup 26
Poached Egg Soup 68
Polish Borscht 30
Pork and Cabbage Soup 14
Pork and Cucumber Soup 69
Pork and Leek Soup 69
Pork and Scallop Soup 58
Potato Soup 14
Potato and Carrot Soup 84
Potato and Celery Soup 83
Potato and Mushroom Soup 68
Portuguese Bean Soup 48
Portuguese Egg Soup 20

Quick Oyster Soup 54
Quick Pepper Soup 72
Quick Tomato Soup 35
Quick Tomato Celery Soup 44

Red Pepper Soup 72
Red Ruby Consomme 63

Salmon Bisque 64
Scallop Soup 36
Scallop and Egg Soup 18
Scotch Broth 33
Shrimp Soup 78
Shrimp Soup with Egg 61
Shrimp Soup with Sherry 53
Sorrel Soup 92
Special Lamb Soup 21
Spiced Cherry Soup 67
Split Pea Soup 35
Swedish Fruit Soup 83
Swiss Gruyere Soup 60

Thick Tomato Soup 89
Tomato Soup 74
Tomato Beef Soup 82
Tomato Bisque 59
Tomato Madrilene 46
Tomato-Salmon Bisque 32
Tomato Soup with Salmon 15
Tomato-Vegetable Soup 71
Tripe Soup 73
Tuna-Celery Chowder 51
Tuna-Corn Chowder 82
Turkish Soup 93
Turnip Soup 93

Vegetable and Herb Soup 62
Vichyssoise 29

Watercress Soup 70

Yoghurt Soup 94